CAPIROTADA

❀

OTHER BOOKS

POETRY

Teodoro Luna's Two Kisses
The Lime Orchard Woman
Five Indiscretions
Whispering to Fool the Wind

FICTION

The Curtain of Trees
Pig Cookies
The Iguana Killer

LIMITED EDITIONS

The Warrington Poems
Sleeping on Fists
Elk Heads on the Wall

A NOGALES MEMOIR

CAPIROTADA

Alberto Alvaro Ríos

UNIVERSITY OF NEW MEXICO PRESS
Albuquerque

First edition
Library of Congress Cataloging-in-Publication Data

    Ríos, Alberto.
    Capirotada : a Nogales memoir / Alberto Alvaro Ríos. — 1st ed.
      p. cm.
      ISBN 0-8263-2093-7 (alk. paper). — ISBN 0-8263-2094-5 (pbk. : alk. paper)
      1. Ríos, Alberto—Childhood and youth. 2. Mexican Americans—Arizona—Nogales—
Social life and customs. 3. Ríos, Alberto—Homes and haunts—Mexico—Nogales
(Sonora). 4. Nogales (Sonora, Mexico)—Social life and customs. 5. Ríos, Alberto—Homes
and haunts—Arizona—Nogales. 6. Authors, American—20th century—Biography.
7. Nogales (Ariz.)—Social life and customs. 8. Mexican American authors Biography.
I. Title.
    PS3568.I587Z474   1999
    818'.5409—dc21
    [B]   99-30583
                                                          CIP

Designed by LiMiTeD Edition Book Design,
Linda Mae Tratechaud

ACKNOWLEDGMENTS

Some of these memoirs appeared in earlier versions in the following journals and books:

Cedar Rock, Connecticut Review, Equinox, Indiana Review, Manoa, New Letters, Prairie Schooner, and *Re/Mapping the Occident.*

The poem "Uncle Christmas" appears in *Teodoro Luna's Two Kisses* (W. W. Norton), and "Day of the Refugios" in *Celebrate America* (Hyperion).

My thanks as well to *New Letters,* the Pimería Alta Historical Society, the wonderful and steadfast early readers of this manuscript, Arizona State University, and my family.

For my mother, Agnes Fogg Rios

❀

CONTENTS

*My mother and father in the 1950s in front
of our new adobe house. Just outside the
photograph is the Plymouth, also new.
Everything was new.*

THE LEMON STORY

When I was about four, or maybe five, my parents bought a new house in what would later become a small suburb of Nogales, Arizona, on the border of Mexico, some four miles outside town. My father was born in Mexico, on the border of Guatemala, and my mother was born in England. From the very start I had many languages.

As we kept driving out to watch the house being built, my mother got to make a number of choices regarding details, among which was the color of various rooms.

My mother, when asked what color she wanted the kitchen, said to the workers who were all Mexican, and who spoke very little English, *limón*. She said it both because she wanted the kitchen to be yellow and because she wanted to start learning Spanish. The workers nodded yes. But when we came back the next day, the kitchen was painted bright green, like a small jungle. Mexican *limones*, my mother found out, are small and green, that color exactly, no mistake.

So that's the color that wall stayed for the next fourteen years, until I left home for college. She said it was a reminder to us all that there was a great deal to learn in the world. You might laugh at first, but after fourteen years you start to think about it.

PART 1

*My father has taken us to one of the
street bars just across the border in
Nogales, Mexico, where anything—
even a tuba—could happen.
We're next to that Plymouth again.*

A ROUGH HANDSHAKE

Nogales in the earliest years I can remember had a smell of woodsmoke in the evenings. The town itself, which is where I grew up, was separated into two parts, the American and the Mexican, by a ten-foot-high hard wire fence. We lived on the American side, in Arizona, but my father's family had lived on the Mexican side as well. I'm not sure what year the fence was put up, but my family could remember the time before it, and still lived as if it didn't exist. They were not alone.

The stretch of land reaching from Guaymas, Mexico, on the Sea of Cortés, to Tucson, Arizona, comprises an ancient region known as the Pimería Alta. It is an old trading route, and people who had families in one part of this region also had relatives in the other parts.

The whole region is high desert, more habitable than the farther central parts of either Arizona to the north or Sonora to the south. There are mesquite trees and shrubs everywhere, a variety of desert curiosities and cactuses—barrel, ocotillo, saguaro, prickly pear—and rolling hills. It is easy horse country, mostly range, with cattle too. Huge cottonwoods signal where the water runs.

As you approach Nogales going south from Tucson, having passed from lower desert and saguaros to higher ground, you can come into town on the I-19 freeway now, but you won't see much. The way into town for me, the way I tell people, is the way I remember it: Take the road that turns left. It's longer, but it's where Nogales is.

Before you turn off the freeway, twenty miles or so from Nogales you will have passed several small towns off in the distance to the left. They used to be on the road, but these days they look more like photographs from the car window. There's Tubac, which is an arts colony and has colonial adobe arches announcing itself. The arches are relatively new, several decades, but the town has been old for centuries.

Then comes Amado, and Tumacacori, with one of Father Kino's missions still strong against the skyline of gentle hills and big cottonwood and sycamore trees lining the Santa Cruz River. This is the heart of the Santa Cruz Valley, which produces among other things its own red chile pepper, whose taste stays with you for life. You can buy some if you go down onto the old road. There's a little shop with a big chile sign.

The river is not really a river so much as the place where a river ought to be. Water runs there part of the year, but you've got to be quick to catch it. The river for most of its journey stays well below the sand. That's where the trees find it, somewhere inside the ground and invisible to us.

On the one hand, the river that runs through the Santa Cruz Valley winds snakelike and S-shaped through the valley. On the other hand, the freeway, with its single-mindedness, goes through that same valley in a straight line. From the air I suspect that as they intersect this must look like so many dollar signs.

Just after you get off the freeway on that left turn, however, and finish the old road's wild curve, on the right you pass by an innocuous piece of land. It's a little swampy on its far edge, and a good place for birds and frogs. It used to be the El Rancho Drive-in, with a towering white screen, all the rows of speakers, the concession stand—which was more like a small adobe house—and a playground at the back. On some nights it was our whole world. At exactly five minutes before the previews would start, they would put a cartoon clock up on the screen, with a minute and a second hand carefully tracking the time. These last five minutes, however, felt nothing like five minutes, lasting for what seemed to us hours. This unforgettable clock helped us understand that nothing was static or absolute in this place, that something like a minute could have many definitions.

❁

On the left you pass by the Highway Patrol offices, and the entry to the old Tucson Road, where I used to ride my bike. There were horses down that road. On that same side you come across a little limestone curiosity, a small half-dome with a statuette inside. This is the monument marker commemorating the passage through here of Fray Marcos de Niza, an explorer and priest. But the statue always looked to us more like a saint.

It was only many years later that I found out we were wrong. He was not a saint—no explorer through here was. His presence and passage here was more complex, and curiously mirrored in a piece of architecture I remember from growing up, and which is still central to both cities. It's not a mission, but rather the biggest and tallest building at the border, on the Nogales, Mexico, side. The building is called the "Fray Marcos," which makes historical sense. At the top of this building, however, was the best-known dance hall and nightclub in town, also referred to as the "Fray Marcos."

This mix of concepts is furthered when considering the base pun of the Spanish word "*fray*," which, when used in "Fray Marcos," means Brother, in the religious sense. Brother Marcos. But when considered in its English language usage, a "fray" of course means a quarrel or a fight.

Still, for as long as I can remember, people have left votive candles at the small roadside monument, and it's where my neighborhood gang put its treasury for safekeeping, sticking the coins in the crannies of the stone. Of course, after awhile one forgets where these places are, and so we never really knew how much money we had.

On the right was the Flagstone Motel and Coffee Shop, though all the things I remember are changed or gone. There's a Texaco station now, and insurance companies that sell policies for travel into Mexico. It's a good idea if you're going to drive there.

Just past this is Valle Verde, a Fifties subdivision we moved to when I was still quite young. This was my geographic life, filled with these houses, which had huge antennas on them in the Fifties, cowfields and cowponds, the arroyo on the left, the horses and hills on the left beyond that. It was a place to grow up.

It was a place where, in the morning and sometimes in the afternoons, you could hear in the distance not the peacocks, but their mates, the peahens, which made a loud and useful watchdog sound when disturbed. This noise would be followed by the cows, which always complained at the loudness of the peahens. The mooing of the cows in turn upset the grasshoppers, which would be startled into their low and desperate flight. This made the rabbits jump up, which startled the peahens and started the whole thing over. It was a show that could go on all afternoon.

❀

Driving forward you pass by the outskirts of town, newly developed all the way to Mariposa Road. This expanse is filled with all the new stores, the Wal-Mart, the McDonald's, the everytown. All the signs here are in English and Spanish, or just Spanish. The stores all run shuttles the three miles or so to and from the border for anyone who wants to shop. People from Mexico used to just cross the line and shop at the stores closest to the border crossing, but these new stores are just like Tucson's stores, and that means something, even here—they're more American.

The signs in Spanish echo something you notice on the drive from Tucson—that all the mileage signs are posted in metric. All the distances you have been reading are kilometers, and so it seems that you get here much faster than you had thought. The feeling is the reverse of how those minutes at the drive-in seemed like hours.

Going toward town, just before you reach the curve of the freeway overpass, you drive by Carroon's Mortuary, and then get onto Grand Avenue, which is a name that sounds like it's

from the Thirties, optimistically evoking those large and for-
ward-thinking ideas of the time: grand, progress, commerce.
Nogales was like that in those days.

Going over the hill at the beginning of town, or where the
town used to start for as long as I can remember before they
annexed north, you pass by Zula's on the left. Zulaburgers!
Need I say more? Since the Sixties, and maybe earlier, they
had a secret sauce before there was such a thing—a secret sauce,
a size, and a taste in the mouth that made the "grand" in Grand
Avenue not ring quite so hollow. Of course, hamburgers themselves as a food were relatively new in town. What we were
tasting was the future, if only in small bites.

At the bottom of the hill, if you turn right you get to the
cemetery, where my grandparents, my great-aunts, and my father—at the end of 1995—are all buried. When I was seven I
remember someone's funeral, and us jumping around the graves
on the cool lawn that was green and shaved, like nothing else
in the desert, running through a hundred lives with our feet. I
know this place well, with its marble laps and grass hair. I know
everyone here.

❁

There's the VFW up on the hill to the right, and on the left you
can see the "N" on a hill in the distance. You drive by the library,
which people sometimes still call the new library, though it was
built in the Sixties. Its architecture strikes a fine and stable balance
between the USS Arizona Memorial in Pearl Harbor and a tilde—
the little mark that goes over an ñ in the Spanish so many of us
spoke, though I think the tilde image was more mine than the
architect's. Regardless, the effect was dramatic. Mrs. Ashby worked
in that library so long that it was like her house, and it's where I
read every science-fiction book ever written.

Science fiction was my life for a while. It's not that I loved
science fiction, but I loved what it showed me: how there was

so much out there. Sometimes as a teenager that's a hard thing to see. Robert Heinlein was my cruise director on this ship, and Isaac Asimov and Andre Norton were its crew. I found out many years later that Andre Norton was a woman, and I was glad. I don't know if it would have changed anything to know that then—that I was reading a book by *a girl*, but who knows. And Tom Corbett, Space Cadet—now here was a guy. With Roger Manning and Astro to help out, what could not be conquered?

Right in this area you can still see the uncovered parts of the Nogales Wash, which everyone calls the arroyo. It's a hard thing to look at these days. Closer toward Valle Verde, I used to play in this same wash. It was my river. But it's not for playing anymore. I've grown up, we've all grown up, the century itself has grown up. Though there are chemicals in the water, some people have to live in the wash now, even kids. The kids—all of them Mexican and trying to find a place in this country, crossing the border underground through the tunnels—come up out of there sometimes, and get in the news for harassing tourists. They ask for money, or take a purse, and then run back down under the covered parts, where nobody else will go. When this started happening, people in town started calling these youngsters "tunnel rats," and worse, even the newspapers.

Standing in between the signs for Jesse's Meats and Maytorena's Car Wash, the arroyo's cement walls are steep and sudden, but looking in that direction you see nothing—it's a trick of the landscape. This thing of not seeing the arroyo at first is our version of what happens when you walk toward the Viet Nam Wall from the high side of the park and how you don't see anything. Then suddenly it's there, and instead of not being able to see it, seeing it is all you can do.

I have seen the Wall myself, the way like cutting onions it brings water out of nowhere. This place, this arroyo, does that too, with flash floods and a roaring echo of some kind of war that forces children to live in there. The Nogales Wash, the way it looks around here, you have to walk up to it if you want to see anything. It's where when we were younger we used to dream about things, but nobody wants to look down there anymore.

And of course we've also got the border wall, which gets all the attention anyway.

❧

Bearing right, being careful not to drive straight into what used to be Garrett Wray's Curios Shop, is the high school, which isn't the high school anymore. It was built out of limestone and wood in about 1912, when Arizona became a state. The houses built originally on the American side were often built from these same limestone blocks dug from a nearby quarry. They are still standing, and there is still a Quarry Street. The old courthouse, built around the turn of the century, was also built out of this limestone block, and was for many years, along with the Catholic church and the high school, a tremendously imposing structure.

This place in front of you may not be a high school anymore, but it's like the minutes being hours and the miles being kilometers. This is Nogales High School, no matter what the signs say on it now.

Just past this, past Walnut Street where my grandmother lived, is the large Catholic church on a steep hill. Standing up there, you can see the steps to the high school, the steps to the courthouse. They were big things, big steps, steps that counted, steps that took some energy. There were back entrances, of course, but it's the steps one remembers.

Right behind the church is Rodriguez Street, where we lived before moving out to Valle Verde. Then there are some stores, leading up to the border. Most of Nogales was built in this pass between these hills, which soon themselves grew houses on them made of things besides limestone. The houses on the Mexican side were made from whatever was available, scrap lumber, sometimes with cement foundations. The colors they were painted, the particular blues and pinks, don't exist on this side of the border, at least not as house paint.

If you turn left, instead of crossing the border, you find the town park and the old stores, the S. H. Kress, Woolworth's, Newberry's, and so on, all on Morley Avenue. All the businesses end at the courthouse, where my father worked for years and which was followed by the post office.

Morley Avenue was the street that had its own guards and border-crossing gate, called the *garita*, that was used mostly by locals. It stopped being a car crossing a long time ago, so travelers didn't come this way often. That meant the guards, who were sometimes Mexican, sometimes American, or sometimes both—I'm not sure it mattered very much—didn't have to put on so much of a show for the tourists, especially since they were all cramped together in that same little guardhouse with no air con. The guards here weighed more, were closer to retirement, were more friendly and wore their ties loose, and they knew us all by our families.

This smaller crossing point is where the two towns used to open up the gates and let parades and people all come through. Cinco de Mayo, Fourth of July—celebrations were celebrations, and belonged to everybody, at least on those days. There was a raised, covered bandstand in the park on the Arizona side, and that's where the mayors all gave their speeches.

❀

The town was founded in the later 1800s as a railroad stop, a station, however impractical in real terms, between two countries. Except for the imaginary boundary line, there wasn't any particular reason to stop in this place. People made up every reason to stop here, however, and that sensibility persists to this day. The place did have a spring, though, and people along the old trade route through here had stopped for the water. This place was called the Cañon de los Nogales, or the canyon of the walnut trees. The town was called Isaacson for awhile after the establishment of a post office in 1882, but the name was short lived, and the town went back as it always had to calling itself Nogales. The park-of-the-mayors-giving-speeches has a small, stone memorial remembering its other name.

My uncle is the mayor now, but I don't think this park is where mayors go so much anymore. The pond had huge gold-fish, and everyone bought popcorn at Kress's to feed them. As a child, it was a wonderful exchange: The fish sometimes made bubbles that came out of their mouths, while the popcorn in the water looked like bubbles going into them.

Water—and the lack of it—is a funny thing in this place. Nogales exists as the southernmost town of the 1854 Gadsden Purchase, though it should not have been. In what appears to make sense of why so much of Arizona settled the way it did, some early accounts of that transaction with Mexico supposed the United States to be purchasing a piece of property that included access to the Sea of Cortés. But surveyors got it wrong. The real boundaries finally took so long to figure out that the papers were signed before the survey was completed the next year, and the missing port by that time was a moot issue. The issue of a water port was never resolved, and the lack of water remains a problem to this day.

From time to time, however, students at the state's univer-sities come up with thesis projects that propose a plan to dredge a canal from the sea to Tucson or Phoenix. It has always been an interesting idea, and one that has worked in other cities, but by now, at the end of this century with not a pick or a shovel in sight, the point is relatively lost. Water is still a hot topic for discussion, but not much more.

The firmness of the border, then, has often been at least a little bit suspect. It has always been, and still is, fluid. Not so long ago when the parades just went right through the gate, it was between hearts as much as between countries. All the drum and bugle corps and the floats and the veterans, both Mexican and American: The fence couldn't stop the sound of the drums, which are still loud even now that—for governmental security reasons, for showing the world that nobody can get across the border, for all kinds of reasons—the crossing parades have been stopped. But anyone who was there remembers, and that memory is big in the heart. What the fence, the wall, stops anyway is uncertain. If the parades don't come through anymore, the music still does. The fence doesn't stop that very well.

There were the parades across the border, but there was the getting-ready for the parades as well, which was just as important. You wanted to make a good impression because everybody would know you. This was the town looking at itself. I remember one woman making paper flowers to sell, with different herbs for stems or decoration. She made them so fast, and so many, and each one different from the one before, that as I watched, her first few zinnias became quickly enough a few hundred, and grew in their happiness to the size of sunflowers. The sunflowers themselves grew to the size of pumpkins, the snapdragons grew ominous, and the rosemary fragrant.

⚛

On the far side of that governmental checkpoint, crossing just barely over into Mexico, was a magical, shadowy street. On the one side was *La Caverna*, The Cave, which was a restaurant built from what had once been a jail carved out of the side of the hill. It once held Geronimo, the Apache. But the restaurant, which was white-linen fancy, became more famous in later years for its turtle soup. My father, for many years involved in law enforcement often pertaining to drug cases, was once almost killed on this street after having dinner.

On the other side from the restaurant was a barbershop called The Three Pigs, taken from the fairy tale. But the three barbers looked like the pigs that were drawn on the wall, at least to me. They were rather rotund men, and quite pleasant. My Aunt Norma took me there for my first haircut, and I went with my father for many years after. I still have a lock of hair from that first time. Next to this there were a couple of bars, the Recreo and the Pitíc. I used to love when my father took me in there because they always gave me a bowl of shelled and salted peanuts.

But the whole way into town you see the border wall. It used to be a chain-link fence, but it's an iron wall now, made of what look like cast-iron sections with little windows. Actually, it used to be an *idea* first, and then a fence and then a wall. I guess it still is an idea.

The physical border with its tremendous fence-now-wall has been elevated into something almost geologic, looking something like a pathetic version of the Great Wall of China, which is reportedly visible from space. But this structure is something else. What we are seeing is a social geography, and while the fence's height may put scaling it out of reach, this only makes the fence all the more visible and present. It is a neat fence along somebody's huge yard, or it is bad scarring on the land, a badly healed appendix incision. Maybe there is something of both those things.

The trouble is, we talk about the border at Nogales as a place only, instead of an idea as well. But it is both *where* two countries meet as well as *how* two countries meet, and the handshake is rough.

The fence at Nogales is no longer a fence. The large wire-mesh sections have all been replaced by scrap-iron panels. There isn't much to say about this that the iron wall doesn't say for itself.

There was some humor at first when the transition in the fence was taking place. People learned to push on a particular iron panel, hard enough and with enough people to make the thing fall over. As it fell it traversed a small canal that ran along the border, and served for a few days as a perfectly good bridge.

But this didn't last.

Crossing the border legally for visiting is easy enough, though the big, new border-crossing building looks imposing and confusing. The structure has been rebuilt several times in my life, and this most recent manifestation doesn't look too different. This new building does the same job. It's hard sometimes to drive across the line—that's what we call going across the border—and some people prefer to walk. There are plenty of parking lots on the American side willing to help out. With so many people parking, however, it suddenly seems like there are so many more people at the border. But it's like the minutes into hours and miles into kilometers and the high school not being a high school: What you are seeing, simply, is all the people coming out of their cars, and while you may see only one car on the highway, there may be six people in it. One becomes six just like that, all around the border.

There was a further extension of this trick, making the town magical in this way: On the American side, as I was growing up, the town's population held steady into the 1970s at about eight thousand inhabitants. But on any given day, forty thousand people were passing through, as tourists, as workers, as people shopping from the Mexican side. On any give day, then, the real population of this town was forty-eight thousand, but the forty-eight-thousand-person town never existed on any census. This was the secret Nogales.

❦

Going across the border into Mexico, one immediately turns right and heads for Avenida Obregón. There are curios shops every single step of the way, with goods placed anywhere they can. Shop workers entice you in with every manner of phrase, and in some form of any language you'd like, so that it sometimes sounds like something from the beginning of *Cabaret*, with a ready "*Willkommen*" and "*bienvenue*," and of course, "welcome, come on in." Tourists come from all over the world to shop here, and to step, if only briefly, into Mexico.

The windows are filled with onyx chessboards and leather vests, with woven blankets and fine *guayabera* shirts, brightly painted tinware and Talavera pottery. *Guayaberas* are formal but common-sense shirts often worn instead of a suit and tie in

Mexico, and they seem like a cross between an African *dashiki*, though not nearly as brightly colored, and a pastel, non-frilly tuxedo shirt. They're usually in easy colors, but in white they are often wedding shirts. Gabriel García Márquez wore one when he accepted the Nobel Prize.

As kids, when we got dressed up for church or for parties, things like that, our parents and our relatives always made us get dressed up in things like *guayaberas*, and we didn't look like ourselves. But that was all right. It was a way for the people inside us to come out, if just for a moment. *You look like your grandfather*, someone would say. Even though he was dead before I was born, it was a small and good way to meet him.

Growing up it was hard to value all this stuff in these stores, because for every one thing there were twenty just like it on the shelf. But now that these things are in my house and out in the world by themselves, I am in love with what I once laughed at.

There's more than goods, though. In Nogales, we're famous for our bargains. But the bargain was never in buying something cheaply—it was in all of us buying things together. And the smell here is different, both good and bad. You smell the cars too much, but you smell the restaurants, too, and the woodsmoke from houses sometimes reaches out for you, offering *menudo* or just-made *tortillas*. Some people beg in the streets, or try to sell trinkets for more than the stores. You buy them anyway.

There is poverty here, but next to the border it's badly disguised with so much weathered crepe paper and forced laughter. The performance is for tourists, but it's not always hollow. If there is laughter, though, it is aimed at life, and not at anything funny. My father was once selling watches on this street.

It's hard to see the real life under this show, but it's there. One need stay only the minute or two longer that stopping takes, and looking up instead of down, or left instead of right, there it is.

❀

People shopped for food at the supermarkets on the Arizona side and at the *mercado* on the Sonora side. But these were just part of how to eat. There was more to learn. The landscape was there, too, and offered itself just as readily: *bellotas*, which were acorns from the scrubby oak trees, the milk-seeds from the devil's claw brambles, mountain onions, prickly pear fruits, which were called *tunas*, the green stuff that grew in our front lawn as part of the grass, *verdolagas*, which I found out many years later was called purslane in this country, and many more. And we always heard you could get water out of a barrel cactus, though we never really tried it. What we did know for certain was that all the barrel cactuses lean south-southwest.

And there was a music, a sound, in nature's store as well, just as rich as the parrots and the crowds in the *mercado*. Dry mesquite pods, for example, which could also be chewed, when hit by raindrops at the beginning of a desert rain made a sound like *maracas*, and played a rhythm those of us who heard it would not forget.

You had to leave the central parts of the town to find these things, though. Turning left on Obregón, you are heading south once again. You pass through the first phalanx of stores only to encounter even more, but they begin to give way, if only slightly. You go by a movie house, and a bakery, where you are likely to stop. The smells work better than any of the shopkeepers' words. You go by the Chinese restaurant, which was called Kin Wah's but which now has a new name.

You don't see them from here, but you can tell there are factories present today. As you begin to go farther you can glimpse the riverbed—which becomes the Nogales Wash on the American side—and maybe parts of the shantytowns that are springing up in service to the factories. The wage is very low, but higher than people can get farther south. This is what people say, and it may be true. The factories are American companies that set up along the border and take advantage of the lax regulations—environmental, bureaucratic, social. This is called the *maquiladora*, or factory, phenomenon, and who knows if it is responsible for Nogales on the American side having the highest rate of lupus in the world, and an inordinate number of cancer clusters. That the air and the water go north, that these have an effect on people, I would only be guessing. But I have three aunts with lupus, and a cousin with bone cancer.

❀

As you start to drive outward from the center of town, things thin out, and you pass two very different statues right next to each other. The first is of Benito Juárez, the first president of Mexico, dressed in Spanish-style clothing symbolic of Mexico's *mestizo*, or mixed, culture. Right behind him, the second statue is much larger and is of an indigenous Indian, representing Mexico's past. The curious irony, however, is that Benito Juárez himself was a full-blooded Zapotec Indian, and not *mestizo* by race at all.

The irony is immediately lost, though, as the larger statue of the representative Indian makes everyone immediately giggle because he is naked. Very naked. The local adults laugh harder than the children, however, because Benito Juárez is pointing toward Canal Street, which is where the prostitutes live.

Prostitution is legal, though controlled, in Mexico. There are regular doctor visits and so on. Canal Street has been, since I can remember, a popular tourist destination, if only in the imagination. When we were in high school, we used to use a code word—"Lanac"—which meant "Canal" backward. We never really said anything about the place because the moment we said its name, frontward or backward, we all started snickering.

I had seen Canal Street for myself, however, and I knew the names and colors of its places, *La Conga*, with its old green neon and mâché palms, with the whistling women at the top of its stairs, sitting where we almost could see them, where they almost weren't shadows. My father drove our whole family through there many times, on one errand or another. I don't know why, but it wasn't ominous. He simply knew people on this street. There were maybe ten places like this along the narrow lane, which was rocky and unpaved. Day and night the street had an eerie shine because of the neon, which was always lit up and reflected in the hoods of the cars that went through.

Across the street from the statues was a restaurant, where we always stopped for *posole*, a pork soup with corn and red chile. You ate this with corn tortillas, not flour—this was one of the rules.

A little farther out you reach the "perimeter," which is an official checkpoint, different from the border crossing. You can cross into Nogales, Mexico, without papers, but to go farther into Mexico, it's at this checkpoint where you present your papers. Paying some *mordida*, some graft, for one small thing or another, even though it has always been officially illegal, was common. It was like giving the official a tip. This, I understand, with the new president, has all ended now.

From here the road leads to Imuris, and then to Magdalena, and then Hermosillo. In the late fall, people would walk the entire distance of sixty miles from Nogales to Magdalena, some of them the whole way on their knees. They were fulfilling promises, or *mandas*, they had made to Saint Francis. I have seen these pilgrims many times along the road. You do not offer anyone a ride, no matter how well you know them. Not even family members.

Driving backward, from Nogales, Mexico, into the United States, you see everything differently. It's like any hike along any trail. You see the other side of everything.

This was a town that's always had one hospital, one church, one high school, but they are opening up seconds now, and the old things are going. There's no news in this, of course. Nothing much that interests the newspapers. But driving it backward, in time and place, I see it, and I see as well what I did not always see the first time.

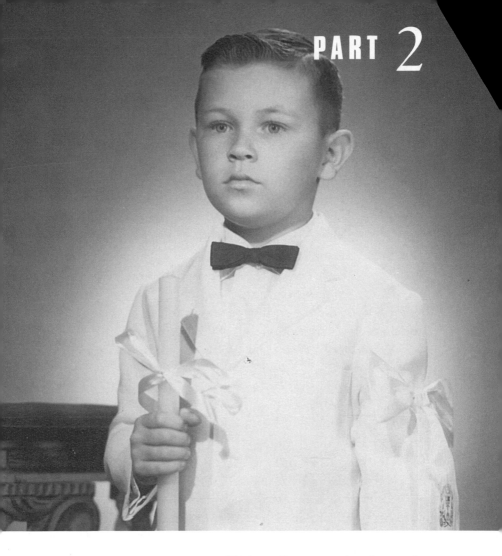

PART 2

*Me in my first communion photograph.
If you grew up in Nogales, sooner or later,
for one event or another, you had your
photograph taken at Tessar's in Nogales,
Sonora. That way, you always looked
good at least once in your life.*

FOUR STITCHES

My first memory is from before I could speak. The setting is clear: It was our apartment on Rodriguez Street. My mother and father and I—my brother was not yet born—had come up the shaky wooden steps, which took several changes in direction. My parents had boxes of groceries in their arms, and I had made my way up the stairs as best as I could.

Our apartment was small, maybe two rooms with a kitchen at the back. My parents had set some of the groceries down in the "living room," and carried some of them to the kitchen, leaving an empty box on the couch, where I was sitting.

As my parents went into the kitchen, I was playing—not one thing or the other, just playing as children that age will: moving my hands around, talking to myself, making a puff of breath. As I looked around, I saw the empty box, and got into it as if it were a car. This part is still absolutely clear to me.

As I sat in the box, I began to rock it back and forth. My parents couldn't see me, or else they would have stopped me immediately. But this all took place in the span of not more than three or four minutes.

Of course as a child the rocking was great sport, and I began to rock the box back and forth even harder. As I did so, a picture formed in my head: It was me, in the box. It was a picture of myself at that moment, but the picture went farther. In it, I saw myself rocking so hard that I rocked myself off the couch, and began to fall to the floor. But, as I did so, I could see myself hit my forehead against the sharp corner of the brown coffee table, and as I hit it my head began to bleed from somewhere around my hairline. Then I landed on the ground and that was that.

No sooner had I imagined the whole scene when it all came to pass, just as I had seen it: I rocked so hard that the box slipped off the couch, I began to fall, and as I fell I hit my head on the coffee table and began to bleed.

As I lay there, I did not scream, or yell, or anything. My parents came in and took care of that part. What happened afterward I don't recall at all. My parents tell me that I was rushed to the doctor, who gave me four stitches. But I don't remember. I simply remember lying there, and thinking that it was all right. That I would be all right. Having seen it all as a movie beforehand showed me.

I don't know what to make of this, except that, even as a child, I knew this was my first memory, and my memory of that moment has never wavered. I had no words at the time to say anything, and I can only imagine how my parents must have felt as they found me there in a heap. But something took care of me that day, something made me feel that this was going to happen but that I would be all right, and I believed it.

To this day I still have the scar that came from the event, and I am reminded of it from time to time as I comb my hair.

I would revisit this moment many years later, but in much more pedestrian circumstances. When I was old enough to ride a big bike, though not quite as big as the bike, I used to ride it perfectly and with great enthusiasm, all except for stopping it and getting off. The bike was a red Western Flyer, and it served me for many years, including when I became one of the first *TV Guide* delivery boys. The theory at the time was that this would work like a paper route, and *TV Guide* came by way of kids on bikes rather than being sold at the grocery store.

I finally developed a plan for stopping, however, and it worked pretty well. We had moved north of town by this time, and as I came into our carport I would slowly glide along the wall, come to a stop, and slightly fall over against the wall's bricks. Then I would climb down from my bike, pull down the kickstand, and give it a small pat on the handlebars.

After a while, though, I started to get a little fancy, and a little cocky. I would sometimes stop before the wall, and come to a stop with my hand leaning on the wooden 6 x 6 post that held up the roof, and which formed the first part of the entryway to the house.

One day, as I came in for a landing, I stopped at the wooden post, put my hand out, but proceeded to miss it entirely, sending me and my bicycle down to the ground, and in the process knocking my head against the edge—the sharp edge—of the post. I got up quickly and brushed myself and my bike off. My head hurt a little, but I hurried to make things right because I didn't want my mother to see what had happened, and then say, "See, I've told you a thousand times." Even if she didn't say that exactly, I knew what she would say would be close.

I took my bike to park it in the garage, and turned to walk back and go into the house. But as I did, on the ground in front of me I saw a trail of blood spots. I took a moment looking at them, and followed them back to the wooden post, where I saw blood on one of its corners, a dark red against the dark brown of the varnish. This all seemed very strange for a moment, until I put my hand suddenly behind my head, and brought it back into view covered with what looked like fire engine paint.

That's when I started crying. And what happened next was like that first memory all over again—rushed to the doctor, four stitches exactly, again, and all the rest. I still have that scar, too.

The events differ somewhat, but they are related as well. There's something inside, something that takes care of us, though I have no name for it. Still, I have seen it, and felt it, maybe not nearly enough, but enough to know. I do not say this with any intent of great importance or to make big bells start to ring. I say this all only as a passing something I am reminded of, every now and then, when I comb my hair.

THE MARCH OF THE ALTAR BOY ARMY

When I was growing up in Nogales we lived right behind the Catholic church, on Rodriguez Street, on a small hill. A curious thing about my mother, having come from England, is that she was Catholic, which was something of a rarity then in that

Protestant country. But she didn't move behind the church on purpose. Rather than religious conviction, no matter how fervent, it turned out to be on account of the Saint of Affordable Housing that we ended up living there.

The Catholic church in Nogales in the Fifties used to do an odd thing, which they have kept up to this day. They would send old Irish priests there to retire, even though the town was maybe 90 percent Spanish-speaking—which as kids we thought was great because, when we had to go to confession, we waited and we went straight for one of the Irish priests, so that we could give our confessions in Spanish, which of course they didn't understand.

We had this confession thing pegged, we thought, but they thought they had this thing pegged, too. They had something like a stop-watch method: How long did you talk? That's how bad you were.

But we got that figured out, so we went into the confessional and talked fast. You could go in there and say the worst thing, forgive me Father, *¡maté a alguien!*, forgive me Father, I killed someone, but say it fast and like it was nothing and you were out of there sometimes with only a Hail—not even a whole Hail Mary. You were out of there. We had this routine down pat, and it was a nice, good, happy relationship.

There's something else about Irish priests. As I've told this story to friends and to people across the country, invariably they have had a similar story to tell, always involving old Irish priests. It's like there's an old Irish-priest factory somewhere, pumping these guys out for the sake of our childhoods and the stories they would star in. But that's just a theory.

The priests in this town finally did just fine. They did their jobs as priests, but as men they were in true exile, in true retirement. This part about the Irish priests was not finally very funny. They had no one to talk to, even after they learned Spanish enough to know what was what. Learning a language is only learning words, which are not themselves the experiences they represent. And even when they later took in more about this place and its people, what they learned was secondhand information.

So, whether as a kid I liked it or not, it made some sense that my mother started inviting them over. They could talk to my mother. They shared some sense of exile, and some commonness of culture, and to talk was a happy thing. A happy thing—except for me. And especially the first time she invited them over.

To begin with, I didn't know at first what was happening. That's what happens to kids, at least back then it's what happened to me. I was supposed to just be quiet. But I could tell that something was up, because my mother fed my brother and me earlier. What, I wondered, what are you doing, saving all the good food for yourselves? Of course, I would never have said this aloud. I liked being alive.

But I was right. My mother set the table all over again, and it was much nicer. And she started cooking something else, which was much better. I could smell that much. When I asked what was going on, she said just to go take care of my brother and be good.

Be good. Have you noticed that "be good" doesn't mean the same thing to a kid as it does to an adult? To an adult it means, don't do anything. Just sit there and, as best you can, cease to exist. To a kid, it's just the opposite: "Be good" means be good, at whatever you do. Good is a good word, and it's what you use when you're doing good things, and good things are loud and wet and messy. That's not the "be good" she meant. I was fairly sure of this.

My brother and I sat by the window, which was our place. We essentially lived in a building with four small, two-room apartments, which is there to this day. To make things fit, everything was combined. Though there were some partial dividing walls, there wasn't really anything like a dining room and a living room or anything else. Things just went where they fit best. A chair was just a chair—never a dining room chair or a bedroom chair. It was also a stool and a toy and a desk.

As I looked out the window on this Saturday afternoon and early dusk, I watched as two of the priests came out of the church still dressed in their cassocks. They looked like they were wearing dresses, but nobody said so. It's that confessions had gone long that day, and the priests hadn't had time to change.

I watched them walk toward our building, and started to say something to my mother, but she shushed me. When I was sure it was our building they were aiming for, I started to say "I think something is wrong with Doña Cuquita, she's sick, it's something." Doña Cuquita was our downstairs neighbor. She was old, and not doing too well. And I knew why priests came to people's houses.

But my mother said to stop it, that there was nothing wrong with Doña Cuquita. I heard them coming up the steps, and thought it was our neighbors next door, then, but my mother said no. And then they knocked. On our door.

I looked around at all of us. Nobody looked like they were about to die.

My mother, who had by this time made a fine meal, and had proven me right about keeping all the good stuff for her and my father, which is what my brother and I always suspected—my mother said *shush* again, and answered the door. As if it were okay.

She welcomed them in, and that was that. Who would know that letting them in was to change my life.

One particular priest came over regularly, and a running routine developed between us. The first time he came over, my mother said, be nice, shake hands with Father So-and-So. Of course, So-and-So was not his name, but that was another thing.

I've asked my mother, and she's told me, but I can't get it quite right. She says something like Father McCaughy, but just try pronouncing that. Add to it my mother's English spin, and I can't even begin to spell it. She says something like "Father McCargy." All my life she added things to words like someone walking into the kitchen might put some more salt in the soup.

I grew up thinking my grandmother was called "Nan-nan," when really what my mother was saying was "Nana."

On the other hand, and just to keep things interesting, she also left sounds out. I was a junior in high school reading a book in class, which is what the teacher had us do when he was exasperated beyond all measure, which was most of the time, and which meant I got a lot of reading done. Well, I was reading a book and suddenly I burst out laughing.

Everybody looked at me, but I couldn't explain. It was mine. I had read a word, which had an apostrophe in it, but at the beginning, signifying that something was left out. The word was "'ell," and meant "hell." My mother must have said "bloody 'ell" every day of my life, and the whole time I thought it was simply some perverse comment on the letter "L," which was my only reference for that sound. After all those years, however, I could see now that it wasn't the letter "L" at all. Not at all.

All of this means that calling the priest Father So-and-So is the best I can do. Those who spoke only Spanish had a different name for him altogether, but stemming from the same trouble with pronunciation. He was Padre Fulano, "Fulano" being the equivalent of "So-and-So." It comes across as something like, that priest over there, you know who I mean. Father Whatever-that-name-is. There was no disrespect in this, and no doubt the priests had just as much trouble remembering our names. The lucky thing for us was, when you met the priest, all you had to say was "Father." That worked out all right for us. The priests, I think, stuck with "my child" for everybody.

Well, be nice, shake hands with Father So-and-So, my mother said.

I was a nice kid. I went right up and put my hand out. He put his hand up, too, but went right past mine and headed straight for my cheek, pinching it hard and lifting me in the process—he had strong fingers—and saying, what a handsome young man you are, while my feet dangled in the air.

The next week arrives, and he comes to dinner again, my mother says be nice, shake hands with Father So-and-So, and so, okay, I put my hand up again. But this time, I bury my face in the side of my arm so there's no way he can get it. He puts his hand up too, just like the last time, and just like the last time it goes right past mine again, but this time, instead of going for the cheek, he goes for the hair, giving it a good, strong, memorable mussing.

This went on and on, and we developed this relationship where, whenever he came over, I'd start circling the room in one direction and he'd move around in the other. I would later see this in wrestling matches on television, which my mother loved to watch, and as the wrestlers would circle each other with menacing intent, I'd think, hey, I invented this.

But one day he came over, and instead of circling around, he just stood there, and put his hands on his hips. He was quiet for a minute, and I just watched. He looked at me, carefully, up and down, and said, "So, then. I think it's time." And he said it in an Irish accent, which made it sound different, and even scarier.

Well, I was still quite young, a little kid, and a priest standing there looking ominously at you and saying "it's time" was pretty scary. It doesn't matter what kind of accent he has.

"What a fine, young altar boy you'd make."

Oh no. Busted. Life as I knew it, I was sure, had come to an end. Altar boy. I knew what altar boys did. I mean, they probably changed their underwear, and took baths. I didn't really know. But they looked shiny up there on the altar. I didn't want any of that—who would—but I didn't know what to do.

I just politely, because I was a nice kid, tried to summon up this "no thank you, Father," but before I could even come close to getting it out my mother jumped right in and said, "of course, of course, he'd love to, Father, anything you say."

And so I was drafted into the Altar Boy Army. If you've been an altar boy, you know that being up on the altar, well that's about five seconds of what you do. The rest of it is, clean the church, and that's what we did, clean the church. It's like you buy five hundred brooms, bring in a bunch of altar boys, and say, that looks like a match. We cleaned, and we cleaned. And we cleaned again.

I really was too young. I learned a lot, though, maybe more than my share. I didn't learn probably what altar boys should be learning in the way they should be learning it, but in the big picture I think I was all right. Something I particularly remember is carrying a very large votive candle one day, the mega-mortal sin size. It was a big, and red, and heavy candle, too much for a little kid. I was walking in, and I tripped in the doorway. The candle fell onto the ground and it broke. But I didn't look down. I looked up.

Because the noise that came out of that candle in that church, that large, cavernous church, was huge—this was my first experience with an echo chamber. And that noise—kapow, wow, wow, wow, ow—it wouldn't stop. That noise is still in the church. It waits for me, every time I come back.

I remember thinking, well, that's kind of neat. And the next thing I did—I knew the priest wasn't there—was the most courageous act I could have concocted at that moment, the most illegal thing I could do. I looked around, to make sure the coast was clear, and I went, "HEY!"

Hey, ey, ey ey. That noise went around and around. You're not supposed to yell in a church, I think, I don't know. It's what I thought at the time. You can't yell, but I yelled. And the noise going around, I thought well that was all right, and I felt pretty good.

I think back now and that was right. It was some way of feeling bigger. It was a big sound that came out of me. It felt good. I remember going back to my friend Sergio, another altar boy who was always telling me things to do in church, and I told him what I had done.

Oh that's nothing, he said, that's nothing. Come over here. And he took me over to the rack of little *manda* candles, which are promise candles. When you make a promise, you light a *manda* candle, at least in the Mexican churches. But the candles all burn at different rates, and that's what was important. They had big candle snuffers lying next to them, and he picked one up and said, listen to this: "do do do be, do do do be," which was a little musical scale sound he made by tapping the glass rims of the candles with the snuffer, from low to high and back down, jazzlike. He knew just which ones to hit, and got a little rhythm going, too.

Hey, that's all right, I said.

Wait. That's not all. He looked at me with a smile. We went back into the sacristy, into the storage area. If you've been to Catholic church, you know that altar boys have these small bells, and a couple of times during mass the altar boy rings them. Ting ting ting. But a little boy with bells in his hands, who's supposed to go ting ting ting—That's not what he wants to do with those bells. So we got some more sets of bells, and with all of them together we went KA-CHING CHING CHING.

We got another altar boy to join us and we spent the rest of that summer, one of us on bells, Sergio on candles, and me on Shout! HEY, ching, do be do be do be do be. It was a rough and loud but sturdy offering, this music, this invented prayer.

My job was the one they gave to the youngest altar boy because you didn't have to memorize anything. You just followed the priest around and held the metal paten under people's chins so the host, as people came for Holy Communion, would not fall to the ground.

The only other thing you need to know is, like with my first experience with an echo chamber, this was my first experience with a carpet. We didn't have any money, and so didn't have any carpets in our house, which wasn't a house anyway. It was an apartment behind the church.

My friend Sergio taught me a real interesting thing about carpets. He said, you know, if you rub your foot a little bit hard along a carpet, you can produce . . . well, I will simply say that I was about to move from music to physics.

Tonio, the other altar boy, had told me at catechism, in whispers, that the big part of the human eye admits good, while the little black part is for seeing evil—his mother, who was a widow and so an authority on such things, told him.

That's why at night, the black part gets bigger. That's why kids can't go out. And at night girls take off their clothes and walk around their bedrooms, maybe jumping on their beds or wearing only sandals and standing in their windows. I was the altar boy who imagined these things, whose mission on some Sundays was to remind people of the night before as they knelt for Holy Communion.

To keep Christ from falling, I held the metal plate under chins, while on the thick red carpet of the altar I dragged my feet and waited for the precise moment: Plate to chin I delivered without expression the Holy Electric Shock!—the kind that produces a really large swallowing, and makes people think. I thought of it as justice.

But on other Sundays the fire in my eyes was different, my mission somehow changed. I would hold the metal plate a little too hard against those certain, same, nervous chins, and I, I would look with authority down the tops of white dresses.

Well, I did it once, anyway. And afterward, I went running back to Sergio to tell him what I had done.

"I did it," I said, "I did it, I looked down Mrs. So-and-So's dress"—there was no relation to the priest—"I looked down Mrs. So-and-So's dress." I said it with great bravado, and I did it, but the truth is I wasn't so sure why.

Tonio might have told me about the eyes, but it was Sergio who had told me how I had the best job in church.

"You get to look down all the dresses," he had said. But he hadn't told me how come. I pretended it was great and said stuff and acted tough, but the truth was it would be a couple of years before I even heard the phrase "birds and bees."

That's why they gave this job to the youngest altar boy, and I really was too young, if only at first. Father So-and-So had done this, truthfully, as a favor to my mother, not because I was trained or ready or had any particular aptitude for the job. It was all right, I think. I didn't think so then, but it was all right, and got better. And I did start to understand about things, enough to know better than to do everything Sergio told me to. Mostly.

THE CHICKEN AND THE BOX

Magicians are fun to watch, and have been for centuries, even though what they do is all a trick, and we know it. We are in awe of them regardless. I think it's because sometimes, if only for the instant, we believe we have witnessed the real thing.

The curious measure, of course, is that we fail to recognize the most obvious notion in all of this: that we ourselves are the best magicians we know. What our bodies do, what our minds accomplish, and the context we can give to things, how we make it all fit together, this is something.

Someone once asked me to stretch my arms out as wide as I could, as if I were going to hug somebody melodramatically or as if I were going to start singing opera. Then, I was to imagine an object about that size, maybe a shovel or a pick.

As I did this, he put his hands on either side of my head, and brought this measure up so that we both looked at the space between his hands—a space about six or seven inches. He put his measure inside my still outstretched hands, and looked at me.

So, he asked, *how do you make a four-foot shovel fit in the seven-inch space of your head?* He was asking me to imagine how a large thing like a pick could fit in a small thing like my head.

Well, the ready and funny answer was, by using my muscles, of course, and by practice and good planning and maybe some folding and some careful inserting through the ear. But we are so good at imagining, we are such magicians, that, by using some nonsense word like "imagination" in place of "abraca-dabra," we make it seem like nothing.

But it's not nothing. Making a shovel appear in the space of a head is something. In this way, we are every day and every moment ourselves the best magicians we know. But nobody pays us. For whatever reason, we are far more willing to pay attention to amateurs.

These amateurs are who we talk about, and what we re-member. And what we talk about most and remember most are not actual acts of magic—like thinking and imagining—but simply the showy attempts at what can't be done. They are things we know are not magic, even if we can't figure them out. So for a while, a good trick stays just that, and you can't do anything but say, that was a good trick.

As kids, trying to do what couldn't be done encompassed practically everything. Getting started, trying to do something for the first time, and coming out of it alive: That was an amaz-ing moment. What if you imagined a shovel and it broke your head open, or poked out your ears. Maybe it could happen. We didn't think so, but who knew, who knew for sure? It's that first time of trying it—that was the dare of childhood.

One of the first places I felt I was growing up, though, was at the municipal all-purpose field in Nogales where the ter-rible Cleveland Indians and the horrible Chicago Cubs would come once a year for a demonstration game, which we all went to, and which invariably never amounted to much.

The good thing was, two teams that weren't very good, playing a demonstration game in pre-preseason with their B-teams or even C-teams gave you hope because you knew you could play at least this well and probably a great deal better.

This field did what I think a municipal playing field was supposed to do. It made us feel stronger by watching, like we owned it, like this was something in our special, personal prov-ince. If this was the world, and these were its players, then things weren't so bad. We were going to be okay. We could do this.

I remember, as a child, standing in that same field with a group of kids in a dirty tent at a carnival that came to our small town. We were watching what must have been a tenth-rate magician who was also probably down on his luck, had the shakes, smoked during his act, and who bathed as often as he shaved, which was maybe something on the lunar calendar. For all of that, he provided me with a moment of magic I would never forget. Maybe it was magic. Maybe it was a trick.

He had a chicken and a box. That was it. He had a few other things to try and distract us—a magic wand, which coincidentally wasn't very straight, a large, silk handkerchief, which was a little greasy, and his voice, which was so raspy and distinct that it had a life of its own, and worked like an assistant for him.

That voice had its own elbows and legs, and seemed strong enough to hold up any tray he might need. I suppose it was beautiful, in its own way, though I didn't think that then. I just knew that when his voice came out of that mouth it was like there were two of him, and that's probably the trick that got us there to begin with.

He introduced himself and his act, and he probably spoke a few words on behalf of the carnival, but I've forgotten all that. He did a few tricks with some cards and some other regular magic things, just like we thought he would, though the cigarette in his hand made the card tricks a little shaky.

But then he got to the live chicken and the box. At first, let me say, neither of them was a chicken or a box to brag about. They both needed paint.

He said a great deal and set up his trick well because he knew we were all listening. We were a little excited and a little bored both, which, mixed together, made a relative equation that allowed gladness to just barely stand against irritation. It was just like watching the Cubs and the Indians play right in this same place. Had we been adults we would have stood there just the same, but we would have been looking at our watches and drumming our fingers against our thighs.

Until he picked up the chicken.

I might point out that chickens don't like to be picked up, and so this was not a little bit of a trick all by itself. The particulars are lost to me now, but what I remember is that, in some combination, he put the chicken—which also had quite a voice of its own, and a vocabulary too—he put that chicken into the box, put the handkerchief over it, waved the wand, and made the chicken disappear. There wasn't any *poof* or cloud of smoke or bolt of lightning. The chicken just disappeared.

Sort of.

He held open the box to show us, and it looked empty, but even then we weren't rubes. Oh yeah, the chicken *seemed* to have vanished, but coming out of the bottom back corner of the box as plain as anything—there was a chicken feather. It was the same color as the recently departed chicken. And it was *moving*.

As a group we yelled and pointed and laughed and said he couldn't fool us, we knew he stuffed that chicken inside that box. We hooted and stamped our feet as he kept trying to tell us something else, kept trying to move to the next trick. He said he didn't know what we were talking about, and tried to make his voice usher us on.

But we wouldn't have it. We kept it up and didn't let him go, so that finally he had to address the box with the moving chicken feather. We pushed him and pushed him with our own voices, and made him finally look down at the feather. And all of us together watched it move.

"See, see, see, see!" we all yelled.

"Oh, that," he said, almost nonchalantly. And we all laughed even more. The feather was the show, and we watched it move again.

But then, all of a sudden, with all of us laughing and in the din of it all, he turned the box around, and showed us the feather—which was just a feather, just like he said, a feather tied to a piece of wire, which was tied to his finger, and which he moved just a little. "Oh, this," he said again, and moved the feather for us.

We were totally stunned. We were quiet and our eyes, if they had been squinting in suspicion just seconds before, our eyes were now suddenly capital O's, all of them, all in a row.

"What," he said. "Did you think the chicken was back here?"

We didn't just *think* the chicken was back there—we were *sure* of it. We were as sure of it as we were of the world. So there we were, sure now only that we were once again kids, and that everything we knew maybe didn't amount to so much.

The magician man's voice crowed louder than the chicken had, and he didn't let us off the hook very easily. He gave us back what we had given to him, all the jeering and hooting and finger-pointing and laughter. It was rightfully ours, and it was like he was just returning a wallet with all the money still inside.

I don't think I learned anything that day. I was still too amazed and wanting to know *so what the heck happened to the chicken then?* But if I didn't learn, I certainly got taught, and down the road the two things eventually met up, maybe too neatly and too much full of whatever begins to make us adults.

I figured out that he used us, our own loud voices, our sure willingness to focus on that fake feather. We were so blinded to anything else that he probably could have sat and read the newspaper twice while we were shouting and we wouldn't have noticed at all. That was a good trick.

But what made it a *great* trick, of course, is that to this day I don't know what happened to the chicken. I know there's an answer, and that if I knew the answer I'd be disappointed, so I don't really want to know, but the fact remains: I don't know what happened to that chicken, and it's something that's stayed with me. He was a terrible magician, this man all those years ago, but he had one great trick.

35

TARANTULAS

The scorpion story is the loudest, about when I was still in diapers. My parents had just given me a bath and diapered me and left me lying on the bed. This was from the days when leaving me meant I stayed there. I was gurgling and cooing and doing whatever it is that holds a baby, whatever it was that held me, and my parents could see me from the other room. It was simple.

There wasn't much choice, of course. Living in that apartment on Rodriguez Street, two rooms—that was about the extent of things. They could see me and they could hear me, and as they saw me and heard me they watched as a scorpion came out from underneath my diaper and walked in that way they do slowly down my leg, the scorpion tail I imagine coming all the way over its brow in some cruel evocation of an Elvis pompadour, all punk and Fifties and swagger and street.

All they can say to me about it is how sorry in that moment they were, how profoundly the moment played itself, how helpless they were. But I never stopped my chatter. As far as I knew, nothing happened more than a chance meeting of two creatures, one moving more than the other, a chance meeting and passing and that was all. This was not so bad, my baby song said. Under my diaper was simply the straightest way to wherever that scorpion was going, and I didn't have any objections. That's the loud story my parents tell.

Or at least the loudest. There's a second loudest.

And it's this, the tarantulas which came later that I remember. I was older, and we had already moved out of town, to the new house with the green kitchen. Everything out there was new, Valle Verde—green valley. They got that right. Green in the middle of the Sonoran desert: That really was new, and not just advertising. Maybe it was exactly that newness, or some charm or some whistle like those whistles only dogs can hear, but it was something that drew the tarantulas to this place.

After the summer rains, the afternoon thunderstorms, which played out like television in the sky, some big panoramic characters dressed in white and black, some good guys and some bad guys fighting it out—after these small dramas cleared away and the afternoon still had light, this is when the tarantulas came out. Not a couple, and not a few. Hundreds of them. Hundreds of tarantulas came out and walked tough-guy like down the wet streets, in which we also wanted to walk, barefoot in the spill and waft of the sky. Everybody and everything wanted time in this place and this moment.

Somebody sometime must have shouted, or been afraid and drawn the curtain and called the police. But I don't remember it. I just remember the tarantulas, and me. We just walked among them, me and my brother and the neighbors and my parents and the dogs and anybody else. We even stopped talking about them after a while. When we walked by them then, we talked about something else, what was on at the drive-in or who had been sick.

Sometimes they made us walk in a kind of hopscotch, jumping a few times on one leg so as not to crush one or be bitten. Sometimes this was circumstance and sometimes it was just our game, to see how far we could go on this living hopscotch street and sidewalk. We didn't always make it, I know, but I don't remember much about what happened if we didn't. Maybe one would crawl over your hand, or you'd make one jump up in the air if you scared it by coming down too fast. Something like that.

There's something else. I don't want to say this because I don't want to believe this of myself, but a few times we couldn't resist. With their backs up, the defensive tarantulas looked like footballs angled on tees, like the stink-bugs that also raised their behinds—and so we kicked them, a good hard kick, so that they flew way up into the air and came down like hands, Oral Robertslike, the way he would put his hand on someone's head every Sunday, fierce and fast and looking to hold on.

I only remember doing it a couple of times, really, and I still feel sorry. At the time, what we thought would happen was that one might start to get kicked, but it would hold on to our foot with those hairy arms. It would hold on and be mad. That was the dare. A mad tarantula. It was something right out of one of those movies we saw every Saturday at the drive-in. We knew it could happen.

These tarantulas weren't all dark colored like they're always pictured in encyclopedias, in browns and blacks. Some of them were orange, orangutan color. They looked the scariest, though it was only because we decided they did. The truth was, orange hair or black hair on the legs and back, it didn't really make much difference.

This went on for a few years, and then we didn't see many tarantulas after that. Somebody told me it might have been a migration, and that seems possible. It was a passing through, like the scorpion through my diaper. And maybe we should have been scared, but we weren't.

THE VIKINGS OF AMERICA

I'll tell you something I've tried to forget. When I was a kid, I was in a gang. We had a terrible initiation to get in, and the thing that's even worse is, I was the leader. I made people do things.

The gang stuff started in my first neighborhood, Rodriguez Street, and I took it with me when we moved. Growing up in the Fifties, where I lived, we weren't boys. We were something else, and it took over part of our childhoods and didn't give it back. We were the Vikings of America.

We said anybody could join, even girls. But it wasn't true exactly, it wasn't so easy. There was a catch. The Initiation. Nobody got out of it. It was scary, and anything could go wrong, but it was simple enough, and there was no turning back once you started.

Okay. Here it is: To join up you only had to do one thing. You had to drink a can of Treesweet lemon juice straight down. Not lemonade, but lemon juice for-real, unsweetened. And remember, this was the Fifties, no insulated lunch boxes. This lemon juice was warm.

Even though we said we had an open-door membership policy, we ended up being a gang of just boys, since no girls really seemed interested in the lemon-juice thing. It took us years to figure that out. Who would have thought that girls wouldn't go for something this great.

The Vikings of America, this was my gang, and I started it in second grade with some membership cards and our own gang logo, which was a V over an Λ with a little o in between.

Now, like I said, I was the president, though that was mostly on account of the other members were all first graders. The gang had two groups, and they each did different things. There was a school group and a neighborhood group, and though they were mostly the same kids, they had different requirements.

At school, there was the lemon-juice thing, of course, which was pretty big all by itself. We did it every Friday, each of us bringing a can of lemon juice instead of a soda or a milk. Then all at the same time we'd take a breath and just say *go* by our eyes getting really big. We'd swallow it down, all at once and without taking a breath, and the even better thing was to snap your fingers at the end if you could, real jazzy, under control, though the truth is we were still learning how to make fingers snap.

But about the lemon juice, it was our version of a tattoo, and it was the without-taking-a-breath part that was the whole trick to surviving. If you stopped halfway, you were dead: The lemon juice would come back up the moment you gave it a chance, and it didn't always care about coming out just through the mouth, either.

We all waited for somebody to mess it up, of course, and that was our entertainment every Friday. You could count on lemon juice. Someone always messed up, mostly because they thought too hard about it all week long. But what happened was, when someone panicked, we all ended up laughing really hard. That meant we'd all end up with lemon juice coming up through our noses, so it was never quite like we picked on anybody. Not with the drinking-lemon-juice part, anyway.

We did pick on kids, though, on the other days of the week. This is what gangs do. It was our job. Usually we did our business on a Thursday, which gave us the first three days to plan and then Friday, with the lemon juice, it just felt like a celebration. This was a rhythm, just like nature.

We picked on kids, all right, but us Vikings of America found our own way. I thought up an idea about halfway through the school year, and it took another couple of weeks to talk the others into it, even though they were only first graders. I guess I was a kind of bully.

What we did was simple. We'd spend the first part of the week choosing who we'd do it to, and then we got to work. On Thursday right after lunch we'd spot our victim, who was usually on the playground or just messing around the trees. We'd wait a little while so we could be sure of what we'd do next.

Then all at once we'd run out, we'd get behind the kid, single file, and we'd start a parade, ten or twelve of us, with that kid in the front. A parade, just all of a sudden like that. And we wouldn't let go. We'd follow along, sometimes quiet, sometimes waving, but mostly out of breath as the kid tried to run away.

They never could, though. We were fast, and determined. Plus, we'd always choose someone we knew we could stay with. For the rest of the hour we'd pretty much parade that kid out, and no trick was smarter than us. We'd carry a flag sometimes, or make some cymbals out of garbage-can lids. Once a guy even brought his father's flashlight.

In the neighborhood group, though, things were quieter. We lived a couple of miles north of town, and there weren't really any kids to follow around, since out there we were all part of the Vikings. In the neighborhood group what we mostly did was carve our club logo into our town's only roadside bench, which was near a little rock alcove with a statue in it commemorating the explorer Fray Marcos de Niza's passage right by here.

When I saw drawings of de Niza and his group of explorers later on in high school, they looked a lot like a parade, too, with de Niza being the guy in front, followed by someone with a flag, then another guy with a lantern. They looked just like our parade. Well, a little.

We kept the Viking treasury in the quartz crannies of the alcove's rocks, and I think it's still there. It was about thirty-five cents when I counted it last, maybe ten years ago. The neighborhood has been annexed by the city, and they've since put a gate and a lock on the alcove to keep vandals away, so now it's hard to get in there to be sure. We earned our money for the treasury by picking and selling mulberries, selling lemonade, things like that.

We hit it really big one week when we started selling candy bars. It was great, and what was even better, it was easy. What we'd do is just take candy bars out of our refrigerators at home and sell them. It was simple, and it tripled and quadrupled our treasury just like that.

Of course when our parents saw what we were doing, a day or two into this grand business venture, they made us pay for the candy bars. After that, we didn't make nearly so much profit, and we finally gave it up. But for a while, we thought we had the hang of things.

What we did with our treasury was always subject to democratic vote among the membership, although it was the same choice every time. The treasury was across the highway from the Flagstone Motel and Coffee Shop, where truckers used to stop. We'd go in with some of our money and buy a couple of strips of extra-pepper beef jerky. That's what it all came down to, those bites of trucker-café beef jerky.

This was the secret of the neighborhood Vikings. When we weren't at school and didn't have all those other kids around and didn't have to drink lemon juice to show off, we figured out that beef jerky was actually a much better idea. Beef jerky and a Coke and a summer afternoon.

We dropped the lemon-juice thing the next year. But after that, the Vikings drifted apart, too. And we wavered a little with our name. We called ourselves the "Iroquois" a few times, just to try it out. Mostly we just liked the way "Iroquois" was spelled, though not all of us could remember how when we had to carve it into something.

First to second grade, second to third, third to what lay beyond. On summer days pretty soon after and for the rest of elementary school we were already nostalgic about the stuff our gang used to do, the parades and the lemon juice. We spent a lot of time those later sixth-grade days sitting around and talking about the good old days. Girls hadn't really come along yet, not girls as girls, and so we were practically like old guys sitting in rocking chairs on the porch.

Yeah, the good old days, we used to say. If it had all stopped right then, you could have buried us happy.

MR. S. H. KRESS AND AUNT MATILDE

It was a place where only five or six panes of glass stood between my mouth and all the mixed nuts in the world. The bolts and spools of yellow and green calico and gingham and grosgrain, the plastic-wrapped lampshades and the smell of popcorn, the buttons and the votive candles, the blond-wood floors that moved with you a little as you walked and which wobbled the thousands of knickknacks enough to make a small noise, a small ceramic noise—this was Kress's Department Store, Nogales, Arizona, in the 1950s and for a while, like this, in the 1960s. It was Nogales, but it was everywhere. Kress's were like that.

It was different at Newberry's next door, and Woolworth's, which—for whatever reason—were always the second and third places you went. And Kress's was not at all like La Ville's, which was La Ville de Paris, pronounced for no reason that was ever explained to us *Paree*, but if you said it like that people nodded their heads. In its early years and because it was more expensive, everyone called it by its whole name, the whole La Ville de Paris, but later it was just La Ville's, which rhymed just a little too much with *the bills*.

My great-Aunt Matilde had worked in both places, but I didn't see her much at La Ville's. La Ville's was a clothes store, and not full of the zoo of wild things that made Kress's. My Aunt Matilde made more sense at Kress's, in the middle of it all. Behind the counter she looked like one more part of the crazy quilt, and she fit tight, right in with everything.

She had been a teacher in some of her first lives, in the small towns of northern Sonora, in Rayón and Cucurpe and San Ignacio. That was a hard thing for me to imagine as I saw her in these later days, my Aunt Matilde half-angel and half-Noxema. But her teacherly self came through often enough, even there at Kress's. If someone ever got too loud, or would argue too long, she would motion with her eyes up at the picture of Mr. Kress, which was not a smiling picture particularly. Something about the way she looked up there, and the way he looked back, something in this was strong enough, every time.

This was the place of "Blue Waltz" and "Night in Paris" perfume, of colored chicks and turtles, and of more lipsticks than anywhere else in the world. This was a place where just having a lot of stuff was not enough—you had to have more. I mean, you might have a whole shelf full of cat figurines, "my cat collection," as people would come to say, you might have a whole shelf like that full of cats but you didn't have this one cat that now you suddenly saw. This was how it was with stores like this. You couldn't explain—you just knew you had to have it. And Kress's was there to serve. To the untrained eye everything might have seemed to blend together, but that wasn't true. This was a place not of generalities but of particulars, even if one had to do a little bit of digging.

Or, if you didn't want to do the work yourself, you could call my Aunt Matilde over. My Aunt Matilde knew the world, she knew the back of her hand, and she knew what was what in this store and what was what in the decade. You might not be able to have a million dollars, but with the help of Mr. Kress and my Aunt Matilde you could assemble a million cats, all of them Siamese. A lot of anything, it seemed to be the way to go. Who could deny the reasoning in that.

My Aunt Matilde always nodded her head in a *yes* when a person picked up a next cat or a next salt-and-pepper shaker. Her *yes* was a comfort, and people came to look for it. To have someone know what you need, however, can be a little frightening, since much of the time you're not so sure yourself. Still, my Aunt Matilde always knew, and without hesitation. I'm not sure she was always right, of course, but I wasn't going to be the one to tell her. I myself knew at least that.

She was the late Fifties, and maybe the first half of the Sixties, and so was Kress's. In this place we were between stores, between countries, and had the added bonus of being able to step into Paree, France, any time we wanted. It made us ready for all of the crossing over we would do, from where we were, up to space travel and beyond. Ready and comfortable.

It would never be space travel, or things like it, that would ever be in doubt. Those things happen. But did the astronauts have thick-enough jackets? First things first was the real science of the world. The rest was easy and took care of itself.

And if it wasn't easy, well, you could always run down to Kress's, find my Aunt Matilde, and pick up whatever you needed.

PART 3

The end of the decade, the end of the Fifties.
A photograph like this was the required
passport out. My hair and my brother's too
was held in place by lemon juice.
It probably lasted a week.

THE FLYING MEN AND THE CENTIPEDE

I first saw the flying men in the 1950s, in the dark lit up with candles. The smoke rose up to them, and framed them too, like angels. It was a hot night, and hundreds of us had gathered at the side of the old Catholic church in Nogales, Mexico. I had seen smoke rise in that church for many years, but now I saw men at the top of where it went, in the sky.

I learned many years later that they were Tarascan Indians from deep inside Mexico, from Papantla, who stood at the top of a fifty-foot pole looking down, maybe at us. It was hard to tell. Some of them played flutes while others took their time binding their ankles to the ends of thick, vine-woven ropes, which seemed to have frays everywhere. They were los Voladores de Papantla, the Flying Men of Papantla, and we were here to see if it was true what they said about them, that they would just jump, and hope.

I would see them many years later, 1995, in Phoenix, but it would be different. Almost tidy. I would watch them check the ropes and know absolutely that the right insurance forms had all been signed. It was in the daytime, and people read brochures about them.

But the first time, it's the first time that stays with me. People did not stay in a circle a safe distance from the jumping area, a circle cordoned off and marked clearly. That first time, people crowded right up to the pole, and the men jumped without testing first. If the ropes now had a nylon sheen, the ropes then anyone could see were homemade. These men back then were not putting on a show.

They were painted, but were not clowns. People pointed, but nobody laughed at them. Their ropes were like fuses, and their thin, reddened bodies, which were maybe painted too, looked like penny firecrackers.

They were faith-jumpers, and it was religion we were in the middle of, religion with sweat and with screams. We were a whole audience in thrall, with blood that—if it came out of one of them—was real because there was no such thing as pretend. These human fireworks were like any, but with the explosions, the green and the blue, the rosettes of sparkle all imagined. But they were easily imagined, so clear was the next moment, the men jumping.

The people watching, my parents, me, we all clasped our hands together quickly, out of instinct. We clasped them together in prayer, but as much in desperation, hoping against hope that these poor men would not explode. *They were Indians*, someone said, and people shook their heads.

What I remember is the sound of that crowd. With so many crowded in, and every last one bringing their hands together in an *oh my God*, it sounded like applause. The sound was inadvertent, but it was there loud, putting this event on a line between what it was and entertainment, whether we wanted to admit it or not.

Real applause followed, but it was the sound of relief, and there was some crying in the crowd. I was young, and heard it all. In Phoenix, so many years later, it was applause, and there were several show times.

This edge between life and death was not relegated only to the flying men in those days, though perhaps they were the angels of its delivery, giving license to celebration as a meaningful outcome, and not simply a day on a calendar. That these men survived meant something.

I saw this edge as a child in other things too. The Mexican circuses, for example, were real. You crossed a line when you walked in, and the many loose screws that should have been holding the audience grandstand were the first circus act you got, if you paid attention walking to your seat. Some screws were clearly in tightly and properly, but some were also in loosely, and as people were walking you could see some of the screws jiggling. I remember seeing one screw pop right out onto the ground, without anybody stopping or even seeming to notice.

This made the ticket worthwhile. If the screws were loose, then who knew what might happen. It opened the circus to the imagination, which was a much better ringmaster. The nylons on the women performers were all torn, the clowns were ruffians, and the large tent swayed as you sat: It gave the illusion of the high-wire artists swinging, though they stood perfectly still. This place and this moment, they were some place to be.

When the men on motorcycles entered the meshed-metal sphere and began to drive around in it, missing each other by only milliseconds and sixteenths of inches, the circus was, if not the greatest show on earth, as the North American Barnum proclaimed, then at the very least the greatest show we had seen, which was even better.

The street parties for *el dieciséis de septiembre* had this quality, too, this potential of palpable danger. The Sixteenth of September is one of Mexico's two independence days, this one celebrating independence from Spain. This meant something. Independence from France, celebrated on the Fifth of May, was all right, and probably got more attention, though undeserved, but independence from Spain, whose language was still in the mouths of this place, this was close to home. It had a different feel, and the parties, called *perradas*, went on for a week, at least.

The word *perradas* derives from something between a pack of dogs and drunkenness, but nobody seemed upset by it. Say *perradas* to this day, and it will bring a sparkle to the eye of the speaker. In that way it is a magic word, a simple word that lets the listener feel something with the heart, which must forget through the years those parts that were bad.

It works that way with me. When I first think of the *perradas*, I think of the fun I had as a child, and later, how we used to drive across the line into Mexico and park by one of the many bars. We'd order *Cuba libres* and zombies, which by themselves as words were remarkable—though it wasn't the words, as sixteen-year-olds, we were interested in.

My family went to a few of those street celebrations in those early years, and I was struck by the rhythm of ritual. Every year someone would assemble the head of a bull out of wires and scrap. Someone else would then hold onto it, or put it on his head, while someone else attached a string of a hundred red, Chinese firecrackers, the kind linked by a lace of fuse.

The fireworks took on the shape of a centipede, or at least it looked like that to my ten-year-old eyes. A centipede on a bull's horns, though—even I could tell that this was a recipe for danger, for something to happen that we could not predict. It looked like a writhing crown, these legs of a centipede on the head of a bull.

The fuse would be lit, and then it was all smoke and fire and imagination. The head in its tangle of smoke and legs could have been anything: the centipede for me, but the ribs of a rattlesnake just as easily, or the contorting fingers of *el malo*.

But for me it was animals I imagined seeing in the head of that exploding bull. As the fireworks went off the head got too hot to wear, and the person would run through the crowd, which squealed. There was laughter, but with burns, a small drink of joy and trampling, nothing in between, and gray smoke. The outcome was not certain. Someone always got hurt. There was crying, but there was more laughing. I didn't know which to listen to, or which way to look.

People always talk about the border as that fence between people there in those towns. That's not the border. It's something else, something underscoring the difference between danger and grace, which is not something that separates people. It's something that joins them, as they face the same border.

The Cold War was out there, and I had seen Sputnik in the night sky, right over my house. We had to take Clorox bottles filled with fresh water to school in case of attack. John Kennedy was still alive. But I had seen Mr. Khrushchev take off his shoe at the United Nations and bang it on the table in an angry gesture, saying he would crush us. It was real enough to even be in his name, or close enough, when we read it in the *Weekly Reader*, *khrush*. We tried to laugh, but this was not a joke.

It's what the flying men helped us understand, and the centipede and the bull, and all the rest. They helped us to understand something that was understandable—Nikita Khrushchev's pounding, anger, the dark, two high school boys fighting behind the gym, one of whom lost a tooth, people dying. It helped me understand my father when he told me he used to jump out of airplanes, but that he didn't want to anymore, even if I thought it was fun. I'd understand some day, he said, but it didn't take so long.

This last time I saw the flying men, I applauded. But that was all. It's not the same now. And I've seen bungee jumpers do a similar thing, and I've seen circuses for years now with my son, but they're mostly identical each time. It's like that with other things, too. Even piñatas used to be something else. Blindfolded kids swinging bats around a crowd of other kids who all wanted the candy—this used to mean something to kids who had none.

I'm not sorry, of course, that these things have changed. But I feel something regardless. I don't recommend danger, or whatever all of this was. I am not comfortable being anywhere near it. But I know I was there in its grasp, in however small a measure. I was there and I am glad it was enough for me. To this day I still do not understand it—that is what I understood. That was not a gift danger gave me, but a grace I took from it.

CIVIC DENTISTRY

I lost a tooth late in grade school, a grown-up tooth, and didn't have it immediately replaced, so I was missing a tooth for a long time. This is an advantage in late grade school and junior high, and sometimes in high school. The unaccountable, untraceable noises that become possible with a missing tooth, these are something. A gap like that is fine, and mixes well with a will to make it produce something from where the tooth ought to be, some ghost moment, some shadow or entry or corner. A noise from there is a noise from where no noise ought to be, and is in that way invisible, yet audible at the same time. This is power.

But after a while, after its use and exercise, after being found out after all and for having been caught and shown up as an immoderate sound glutton, but hero in the process—after that, then missing a tooth becomes more regular, more just missing a tooth. It goes from something right to something wrong, and for no particularly good reasons. What happens, I think, is that in high school you just end up looking in the mirror a lot more.

And you realize, like it or not, now that the carnival ride of junior high school is over, you've got to go to the dentist. Again.

But years earlier it was the dentist that got me into my toothless predicament in the first place.

We didn't have much money, and who says you can't trust the Mexican doctors anyway we all said, and so there we were. I had a toothache, and my parents found a dentist across the border, in Mexico. He didn't cost too much, and was the friend of somebody.

His office was in a reconverted government building, which was relatively new but already cracking. The arrangement was part of a government program to ensure that all buildings and all spaces got used. It was also part of a greater notion that something like getting your teeth fixed was part of your civic duty—pay your bills, go to the movies, vote, get your teeth fixed. It was a progressive civic view. Plans like that always make sense for a while.

If only getting your teeth fixed actually felt the same as paying a bill, if only that were true and not just a joke, then the plan would have worked. I remember walking up the grandiose, governmental steps, going through the large, glass doors, then walking down the oversized hallway. It was big in everything, the way government buildings in the old style always are. Big to be impressive, and therefore to assert authority. But big so that they always had heating and cooling problems as well. There was a little bit of the Wizard of Oz in all of this— don't pay any attention to the man behind the screen.

I remember that as we reached the dentist's office, and as I sat trying to be good and brave in the small waiting room, I could hear a little boy screaming. We sat, but for me it was like sitting on a big spring, so that the chair kept pushing me up and hurling me toward the exit.

When we were finally called, it was the dentist himself. He was sad-looking, even his body seeming to have an apologetic posture. I think now about the high suicide rate for dentists, and when I read those statistics I always think of this man. He did not wring his hands in a gesture of discomfort, but it's how I remember him in the moment. He might have said he was sorry for keeping us so long, but I understood he was sorry for more than that.

And then I entered the room. Like everywhere else in this building, it was a huge room, unused, except for the dentist's chair right in the middle, with a spotlight illuminating it. The proportions were immediately dreamlike, everything either out of size or else so circumscribed as to be underlined to the eye—the spotlight lit up the chair and made everything else dark by how much light it gave off in that one place. This was a scene from a movie, a bad movie, one that would repeat for me many times in dream.

I don't know how I was cajoled into the chair, except that I was a very nice boy, willing to go even this far. It was an act of love by everyone, and an act of hope—that this would be a good idea.

Because the room was large, the instruments echoed. The dentist, I remember, sweated. He was very nice, and nervous everywhere in his body, except—and this was a small gift in the moment—except in his hands. My tooth was impacted, and would have to come out.

I don't remember very much about what followed, except that if the instruments echoed, what I felt echoed as well—the pain, but the fear even more. I knew then that this was a moment for memory, and in that way I already was not there.

Something inside me took care of me. I don't have any other way to think of it. My tooth got taken out, no decision was made about what to put in its place, and we left.

My parents took me to the corner drugstore, which I always remember as being one of those buildings that used its corners. It was v-shaped, extending itself out at a perfectly sharp, acute angle as two streets made a curious X right in front of it. The building would not be daunted, and cut into that intersection like a wedge of pie. We sat in a booth next to one of the windows and they ordered me French fries. It made me feel better.

My mouth bled a little that night, but not too much. And that's how we left it. I didn't get a bridge until after I got out of high school. I might have already been in graduate school. That's also how long it was before I went to a dentist again. My first and second visits to the dentist, with only twenty years in between.

The next time I went, it was my own idea, and on my own terms. I still didn't have any more money than my parents, but I did have more to say. This time I recognized that the cost was not about money, but about something else, about fear, and twenty years, these were the measure. Civic dentistry is a good idea on paper, but a different thing altogether in the dentist's chair. This time I chose a dentist in Tucson, with a very small office and instruments that *whirred* rather than rattled. I didn't suppose he would do anything much different, but at least there wouldn't be any echo.

Waiting so long was not smart, because when I finally did go, the dentist had to chart out a several-month plan of the work he needed to do in my mouth, a plan that included a miner's hat, the kind with a flashlight attached, and a pickax. Waiting was not smart, but it was not stupid, either.

THE BIRD-MAN

A man we called Bird-man, who was a trapper and a prospector and who knows what else, used to come down from the mountains for a month or so every year. You never missed him for all that time he was gone, and always knew him when he came to town, as if he were always there. He had a way of just fitting in, which is what must have made him a good trapper: no noise, nothing big, nothing new. He was just always sitting there one day, looking down at the paper or staring out—not blankly, but studiously, so that you always thought there was something out there.

The thing about him was, which makes you wonder why he got the name he did, is that the Bird-man wasn't a bird so much—he was more like a beaver.

He had a ponytail. But this was not a regular ponytail from the Sixties, not a ponytail for show or for fashion. It was more. It was a personal ponytail, something more defining and lasting. A personal thing is different, and all the books and all the magazines in the world can't tell you what that is. Through the years he had left it alone, uncombed and ragged, pulled together but only a little, only as much as he could after so much time. It matted itself and made grease. It had a low-order shine and a solid look, as if the hairs were more etched on than actually there.

Still, everybody called him the Bird-man. I don't know why. I think maybe he got called Bird-man because he wore a feather sticking out of that ponytail, and from the front that's what you could see better than the ponytail, the feather. In truth, I don't know if he wore the feather or if it had just gotten stuck there, and he couldn't get it out.

If you didn't look at him any more, that's all you saw, the tail and the feather and the fur clothes. And that's exactly what happened with a lot of people in town. They looked at him once, for a moment, but then they wanted to look at something else. He had a way of disappearing into his beard and into his clothes, and people had a way of letting him, and that was okay all around.

This was all the opposite of the War-man, who also walked around town. Nobody wanted to look at him either, but he looked so hard he saw things that nobody else could, and what he saw was stronger than what they didn't see.

It was his men, his troops, and somehow he got stuck forever with them, in a very long hour. Nobody could see the men except him, and all he did around town was keep turning around and waving at them to follow him.

Sometimes he had to shout at them because they didn't want to come along. He had to shout, loud, and call a few of them out. But it was clear there wasn't much time and so he didn't have much patience in all of this. It was not good to be around him then.

Most days, though, he would turn and wave, and they would follow, maybe ten times an hour. That was the War-man.

Bird-man, he only saw what was there in front of him, for real, and it was the same as what we saw. He didn't pay attention to much else, and he spent most of his time drinking coffee at Denny's. But if he couldn't see things that we couldn't, he certainly could do things that we couldn't, and eat things that we wouldn't. And so on. That beaver tail didn't just come out of nowhere. It meant something—we knew at least that much about the world.

One day we decided to follow him after he left Denny's. It was a simple enough plan, and something to do on a summer Thursday. War-man had his own men already. We'd be Bird-man's guys, somebody said. Bird-man's guys more or less. We hadn't really thought it out that far yet. Mostly we decided we'd just follow him first and see what happened.

That tail meant he was part animal, so we didn't know what to expect. The one thing we should have known, though, given everything we knew about him, was that he would know about us. A small group of boys trying to do anything together is not very quiet, even with all of them saying *shhh* and *quiet*. Saying *shhh* and *quiet*, though, are pretty much the opposite of *shhh* and *quiet*.

But suddenly it was like a little pie slice of time and space got cut out of what we were doing, right in front of us, so that what was in front of us got picked up somehow and was put down in back of us.

What I mean is, there he suddenly was, walking right behind us just the way we were walking right behind him. What we were doing was okay, of course, but for him to do it, well that was a whole other thing. And how the heck did that happen anyway was a pretty big thing in our heads that moment—like somebody had just slapped us, that big.

Oh Jesus, somebody said, and somebody else started to run. One thing led to another, so that we got out of there, all of us, just as fast as we could—including the Bird-man. We ran and fell and shouted in one direction, and he just disappeared in the other.

It was all spooky, and when we finished talking about it the Bird-man was seven feet tall and had teeth that looked like nails coming out of his gums. Stuff like that. The more we talked about it, and the more sure each of us was of our story, the less we knew. Somebody finally said that maybe it didn't even happen.

What, like a dream? Don't be stupid.

The problem was, the next time we all showed up at Denny's, and the Bird-man was sitting there, we didn't know what to do. But the Bird-man did. We spent the rest of the day trying to decide if we should go in and say to him *hey what's the big idea of following us*, but then somebody said *weren't we following him*, and *oh yeah*, and so on. But the Bird-man knew.

We came in the next day, and he was gone. We still hadn't quite decided what to do, but we knew we had to do something, and suddenly now we didn't. He had done it to us again.

Now don't get me wrong. We always liked him, and I think he always liked us, and none of this was bad, exactly, it was just spooky. That's something else. It was just spooky. We still say that when we talk about him even now. The Bird-man, the War-man, those guys, and that day we tried to find out something. I don't know if we did, though. Maybe that was the point. Maybe it was something about what's personal. I don't know, but it's lasted a long time.

THE SECRET LION

I was twelve and in junior high school and something happened that we didn't have a name for, but it was there nonetheless like a lion, and roaring, roaring that way the biggest things do. Everything changed. Just like that, only nobody could tell. It was like the tablecloth those magicians pull where the stuff on the table stays the same but the gasp! from the audience makes the staying-the-same part not matter. It was like that.

What happened was, first, in junior high school we had teachers now, not just one teacher, the way we had the year before and every year before that. Now it was Teach-erz, and though we had no real words to say this, we felt personally abandoned somehow. At least I did. The change just happened, and we were supposed to go along.

But what happened was, even though we had all these teachers now, we didn't get taken care of the same way—even though six was more than one. Nobody really had to do anything for us because somebody else was supposed to. That's what it felt like. Six was more than one, all right, but I don't know what it taught us. Our arithmetic added up in a way different from what it was supposed to.

And we saw girls now, or still—like we always did—but they weren't the same girls we used to know because we couldn't talk to them anymore, not the same way we used to. Certainly not Sandy. This was true even though she was my neighbor, too. I couldn't even talk to her. She just played the piano all the time now, and studied, and said once I was being silly about something. There was something about the way she said it to me. I think she might have been right.

And there were words, oh there were words in junior high school, and we wanted to know what they were, and how a person did them—that's what school was supposed to be for, after all, learning how to do things. Only, in junior high school, school wasn't school. Everything was starting to seem backwardlike. If you went up to a teacher and said the word you were curious about, you got in trouble for saying it.

And don't even think about learning to do it.

So we didn't say anything, my friends and I. At least the boys. We just shut up, all of us, at least about things that mattered anyway. All we could do about girls was be silly. And we figured it must have been that way about other things, too, not just talking to girls, so we never said anything about anything, not in class, not at home—we weren't stupid. We had learned.

❁

But my friend Sergio and I, we solved junior high school. We would come home from school on the bus, put our books away, change shoes, and go across the highway to the arroyo. We did everything just like we always had, except for the last thing—going to the arroyo. It was the one place we were not supposed to go. So we did. This was, after all, what junior high had at least shown us.

There was water down there, though, and trees. It might have been just a little stream, really, the Nogales Wash, but through the months it became our river, our personal Mississippi, just like we had read about. Though we couldn't say so, not aloud, this stream became our friend, because we could talk to it. And the arroyo talked back. It was full of its own stories and happy to hold all the branch forts we had built in it before we got told to stop going down there.

My friends and I had first discovered this place when we were a couple of years younger and still calling ourselves the Vikings of America. We had our own symbol, which we carved everywhere, even in the sand, which let the water take it. That was good, we had decided. Whoever was at the end of this river would know about us.

Now when we went down there, Sergio and I, we had a different plan. At the very very top of our growing lungs, what we would do down in the confines of that arroyo was to shout every dirty word we could think of, in every combination we could come up with. And we would yell about girls, maybe even louder, and all the things we wanted to do with them. We didn't know what we wanted to do with them, just things. It was all right and not scary.

We saved the scary things for when we yelled about teachers, and how it's true we loved some of them, like Miss Crevelone, but it was mostly how we wanted to dissect some of them, and we'd make slash marks in the air to show how. That didn't last, though, because our hands moving through the air finally looked like we were making signs of the cross, like priests, and it scared us too much. We had been altar boys together, after all.

But we would yell all the rest of this stuff over and over because it felt good. We couldn't explain why, and didn't try. We just knew it felt good and for the first time in our lives there was nobody to tell us we couldn't. So we did.

❀

When I was five or so, we moved away from where we had been living in Nogales, on Rodriguez Street near the border, to this place about four miles north of town, on the old Tucson Road. Sergio's family was already out here. Out in the wilds. Or at least the new place seemed like the wilds because everything looks bigger the smaller a man is. In this new place, instead of a border fence, we looked across the highway in one direction and there was the arroyo. Hills lifted up in the other direction—or mountains, if you were a small man.

When the first summer after moving came, the very first place we went was of course the one place we weren't supposed to go: the arroyo. Five years old or ten years old, it didn't matter—the arroyo was always a magnet. To this day it calls out to me as I drive along its obscured banks. I can't see it, but I can hear it. That first summer we went down there and found running water, summer rainwater mostly, and we went swimming there the second summer.

But every third or fourth or fifth day, the sewage treatment plant that was, we found out, upstream, would release whatever it was that it released. We would never know exactly what day that was, and a person really couldn't tell right off by looking at the water, not every instance, not so a person could get out in time. We went swimming that summer and some days we had a lot of fun. Some days we didn't.

Since we weren't supposed to be down there, on those days we got covered in sewage we found a thousand ways to explain what happened, constructing elaborate stories about the neighborhood dogs, and hadn't she, my mother, miscalculated her own step before, too? But she knew something was up because we'd come running breathlessly into the house those afternoons wanting to take a shower, even—if this can be imagined—in the middle of the day.

Today there are signs posted everywhere saying to stay out of the water, and not to drink it, and similar exclamation-point signs. The water comes now not so much by way of the wonderful summer storms of July and August, or even from the sewage plant, but from underground, from the seepage and discharge of the *maquiladora* factories just over on the Mexican side of the border. The last time I went down into the arroyo, a small drop of water splashed onto my wife's blue jeans and bleached a white spot into them.

It reminded me of my mother several years ago talking to me about her water, which comes from a nearby well. I asked if she thought there was anything wrong with it, given all the signs near the arroyo.

No, she said, it's all right. As long as you let it run for a minute or so, the brown stuff all goes away.

❖

Sometime around that second summer was the first time we stopped going to the arroyo. Getting dirty the way we did taught us to look in the other direction the next year. We decided, as the next summer came, we wanted to go into the mountains. They were still mountains to us then as eight-year-olds, though they were really the rolling hills of the high-altitude Sonoran desert, hills ants could have made.

My friend Sergio and I went running one summer Thursday morning—we always started these things on Thursdays— into my mother's kitchen, and we asked her, well, what's in those hills over there out the window? We used her word, *hills*, so she'd understand us, even though we could plainly see they were mountains.

She said, "oh nothing." We left the kitchen, but we weren't dumb. As we left we thought with our eyes to each other, ah, she's trying to keep something from us. We knew about adults.

We had read the books, after all. We knew about bridges and castles and wild, treacherous, raging, alligator-mouth rivers. Real rivers. And we wanted them. And we knew they existed in mountains. And those were mountains, no matter what anybody said. So we were going to go out and get them, like explorers.

We went back into the kitchen and we said, "We're going out there, we're going into the hills, we're going away for three days, don't worry."

She said, "All right."

"You know," I said to Sergio, "if we're going to go away for three days, well, we ought to at least pack a lunch."

But we were two young boys with no patience for what we thought then was mom-stuff: making sa-and-wich-es. My mother offered no help beyond shaking her head. We got our knapsacks that my mother had sewn for us, and into them we put the jar of mustard. A loaf of bread. Stuff. Lunch. Knives, forks, plates, bottles of Coke, a can opener. This was lunch for the two of us, and looked pretty good. We decided we'd put it together when we got where we were going.

The trouble was, we were so weighed down we had to hump over to be strong enough to carry this stuff. But we started walking, anyway, into the rising distance. We were going to eat berries and stuff otherwise, as snacks. We had already discussed this.

"Goodbye." My mother said that.

After the first hill we were dead. But we walked anyway, mostly because we knew my mother could still see us. And we kept walking. We walked until we got to where the sun is straight overhead, noon. That place. Where that is doesn't matter—it's time to eat.

The reality is we weren't anywhere close to that place. We just agreed that the sun was overhead and that it was time to eat, and by tilting our heads a little we could make that the truth.

"We really ought to look for a good place to eat."

"Yeah. Let's look for a good place to eat." We went back and forth saying that for fifteen minutes, making it sound like lunchtime. We always said the same thing back and forth before lunchtimes at home. As we walked we started our ritual. "I'm hungry all right," I said, and nodded my head. Then Sergio said, "Yeah, I'm hungry all right too. I'm hungry," and he nodded his head. I nodded my head back. After a good deal more nodding, we were ready. This whole interchange finished itself just as we came over the top of a little hill.

We were still walking, but we stopped right there, because on the other side of this hill we found heaven.

We looked at it. It was just what we thought it would be.

Perfect. Heaven was green, like nothing else in Arizona. And this was Heaven, not a cemetery which was the only other green place like this, because we had seen cemeteries and they had gravestones and statues that this didn't. This place was perfect, with trees—so many trees—and birds like we had never seen before, not so many in one place.

It was like "The Wizard of Oz," when Dorothy and the others got to Oz and everything was so green, so emerald, that they had to wear those glasses. And we ran just like them, laughing, maybe looking around to make sure there weren't any of those poppies they had in the movie. But there weren't, and we started laughing in that moment, really crazy and happy, and we went running down to a clearing in it all, hitting each other that good way we did.

We got down there, we kept laughing, and we kept hitting each other. We unpacked our stuff, then started acting "rich" because we didn't know what else to do. We knew all about how to do that, like blowing on our nails, then rubbing them on our chests for the shine. Putting our hands on pretend vests. Surveying our very green domain.

We finally got down to business, making our sandwiches, opening our Cokes, getting out the rest of the stuff, the salt and pepper shakers. We had pretty much brought everything. I found this particular hole in the grass and I put my Coke right into it, a perfect fit, and I called it my "Coke-holder."

I got down next to it on my back, because everyone knows that rich people eat lying down, and I got my sandwich in one hand and put my other arm around the Coke in its holder. When I wanted a drink, I lifted my neck a little, put out my lips like I was kissing really big, and tipped my Coke a little with the crook of my elbow so that it went mostly right into my mouth. Ah.

We were there, lying down, eating our sandwiches, laughing, throwing bread at each other and out for the birds. This was heaven. We had done a good job of imagining it. We were laughing and couldn't believe our good luck. My mother *was* keeping something from us—ah ha—but we had found her out. Grown-ups never wanted you to do anything or go anywhere. Well, forget that. We even found water over at the side of the clearing to wash our plates with. We had brought plates.

We ate fast, even though we tried to be slow. Sergio started washing his plates when he was done, and I was being rich with my Coke, and this day in summer was right—was a light breeze and a green hum.

Suddenly, two men came from around a corner of trees and out of the tallest grass we had ever seen. They had bags on their backs, leather bags, not like mailmen's bags but longer, and full of tools.

We didn't know what golf clubs were, but I learned later. The two men yelled at us. Most pointedly, one wanted me to take my Coke out of my Coke-holder so he could sink his golf ball into it.

As they waved and waved and yelled at us, something got taken away from us that moment. Heaven. We grew up a little bit, almost in a lurch, and couldn't go backward. We *learned*, which should be a good thing, but sometimes it's a little uneven. No one had ever told us about golf. They had told us about heaven. But we had to give it away, and got golf in exchange.

❀

Sergio and I and some of the other kids in the neighborhood went back to the arroyo for the rest of that summer, and tried to have fun the best we could. We hadn't gone looking for golf, but we almost knew it would be there—we were two boys in the world and not stupid. We knew things got taken away.

It's just that this was big. What we felt readied us for the yelling we would discover later. It got us ready for junior high, and whatever lay ahead. We didn't tell our mothers, or anyone else, but it was all Sergio and I talked about, for a long time, till we forgot. Golf was the lion, one part of the lion, one of the hundred million things we imagined out there just beyond us, and which we would find out.

The lion was how we felt giving so much of ourselves, giving up heaven, for this news of the world. The roar of the lion we heard came, finally, from somewhere much closer.

It came from us.

YO SOY NEGRO

"Yo soy negro
yo soy negro . . . "

The Rodriguez Brothers sang the Spanish words to this song, *yo soy negro*, as a kind of blues and a kind of lament and a kind of show, if the lives of anybody can be a show. These repeating lyrics weren't written, they just always were, *I am black, I am black*. The Rodriguez Brothers, at the Newport Folk Festival, 1962. Who would have thought it? Who would have invited them, and why would they have come. Who would have heard of them, all scraggly toothed and old like they were, mumbling out what they had to say and then laughing. Laughing every time like the joke was dirty.

It was July of 1970, and 1962 had long passed, but this was one of only a couple of tapes lying around that I could listen to as I worked a summer job before going to college. I listened to the tape so many times I knew the songs word by word from beginning to end, and even began to think about them as I sang along in the empty store.

When the Rodriguez Brothers half-talked and half-sang their song they drew out what was there in it—*yo soy negro, yo soy-y negro*. I am black, I am and black, playing on the small sounds, which are not small in that language of a song being sung or a word being said. *Yo soy negro, y oso y negro*, I am black and bear and black. Each nuance made itself, putting itself there. The Rodriguez Brothers could make the letters of the language move around—that's what those snaggle teeth of theirs did. They didn't let the words come out right or the same way twice.

There were other singers on that tape. Buffy St. Marie and her song "Co-dine." Co-dyin, code eyein. It was a season of sounds, of the something between letters and the still-inside voice.

I didn't hear this music until several years after that particular Newport event. I remembered 1962 was the year, I think,

Bob Dylan got booed off the stage for walking on with a guitar he had officially made electric—I say officially on account of he had to plug it in. But that was just a formality. It was always electric.

That moment—I wasn't there, but I had read about it and listened to Dylan so much that it felt like I was—that moment still had energy for me in 1970. I was working just before and just after graduation from high school in a frame and art supply shop, where I didn't get paid exactly—I just got to get what the shop had. I was painting then, and the art supplies were something. And the owners let me show my things in the shop, though it didn't do much good. Nobody ever really came in, and I don't know how the shop stayed open as long as it did. But this was the late Sixties. A lot of things happened that I couldn't explain.

The owners were hippies, which should have made them all right, but they were absent landlords too, and using the cheap Mexican labor across the line. That's where they got the frames. I didn't know how to feel about that. It was a simple deal, really—they just brought the frames across the border from the Mexican side to the American side and then charged more. And people bought the stuff.

They did a lot of mail-order business, too. They took better pictures of the frames than the Mexican workers did, I guess, and made a better catalogue. The whole thing wasn't much, and I didn't get what any of it meant then. Cheap labor, exploitation, labor issues—these were all ahead of me. All I knew is that it was where I worked. Though, did I already say that I didn't exactly get paid? Well, at the time, that was all beside the point.

That frame shop itself had a smell that was wood and finish and a little more. It's still what I think of when I think of the real late Sixties. That and the Volkswagen. Tan color—I never could figure out why anyone would want a car that color, especially if they were in the art business, even tangentially. I should have paid better attention. But it was a great car and had a sun roof, the kind that opened with a handle.

They left me in charge of the car, too, for a week sometime that summer. I didn't have much of a car myself, and this was some big thing. I remember two events: It was raining that summer and I drove around a lot with my friend Paul. The first thing I did when I got the car was pick Paul up, open up every window, and cruise. That's when I learned the first thing. Passing a semi truck in a Volkswagen after a lot of rain—it gets a fellow wet.

We spent the next two days working at the car with blow dryers, and riding around with soggy jeans. But who cared. It wasn't until the day before I was to return the car that I noticed the odometer. It's amazing how big that odometer looked in that small car.

We spent the rest of that afternoon with the car on blocks and us running the thing in reverse. It didn't do any good, as I remember. I just finally returned the car and didn't say anything. And they didn't say anything. I still feel weird about it.

I painted while I was in the shop. It didn't really last. At the same time, I listened to music on the owners' cassette player. Cassette players were new then. They had left a few tapes in the shop, and I played them all the time. There was the theme from "Topkapi," a homemade tape of odd mixes. And the *Newport Folk Festival, 1962*. I didn't know then why they had something like that—why didn't they have the Folk Festival from 1969 or something, something closer. Even when I played it I didn't understand. What's even harder to understand is that I later bought that exact music as a record album, and played it repeatedly as well, even several decades later. The album jacket is where I saw an actual picture of them, and it was just what I had imagined.

But it wasn't to understand. That was the thing. It was more like the smell of the store.

I always come back to the Rodriguez Brothers. I think it's because they always come back to me. I find this hard to explain, and I'm not entirely sure why I picked them out to listen to or why I remember them in the first place. But I know there weren't very many albums or much of anything else that called to me in that small town. Rodriguez, though—I knew that name. I lived on that street.

I found my way to Roberto Clemente and the Pittsburgh Pirates for maybe the same reasons, Clemente and others. But I didn't think about any of this much. It's just that the Rodriguez Brothers, wherever they were from, and Roberto Clemente and everybody else who had something I knew about: They sang, all of them, and I listened. It was something more than entertainment. It was a conversation, even if I just tapped my foot and nodded my head a little in the listening.

PART 4

*My parents on their honeymoon in
Guaymas, Mexico. It is a desert beach,
spare and cool at the end of October,
1951, each of my parents taking turns at
the camera, looking at each other in
all the ways they could.*

DAYS WITH NAMES

Some days have names, something beyond Monday or Wednesday—we call them holidays and anniversaries. Some days, though, are just as important, and don't have names at all. Both kinds have a life inside our lives, and help make a calendar of meaning. Named or not, that's what holidays are: They are us stopping to remember ourselves.

My own calendar—my own sense of time as well—starts with my father and mother. My father was born in Tapachula in the state of Chiapas in Mexico, on the border of Guatemala. My mother was born in Warrington, Lancashire, England, in a town bordering Liverpool and the Beatles. I was born in Nogales, Arizona, on the border with Mexico.

I come, clearly enough, from a home full of places, languages, and cultures, and one might suppose that I come also from a home full of holidays. And I do. But mine are bargained holidays, composite beasts, a little from this side of the border, a little from that, a little from this side of the ocean, a little from there. I don't have more holidays, really, just stranger ones. They belong in this way only to me, and to my immediate geography, nothing so perfectly American, or Mexican, or English, or anything.

The Fourth of July, a holiday we know well, more or less, is the best test and the best example of what is mine. I lean toward thinking of events like the Fourth of July as metaphor: a sky full of striking colors over Arizona, while at the same time how much scary noise that makes, this confusion of perspectives.

This time has made itself into a poem for me, called "Day of the Refugios." It's my Fourth of July poem, though it's a stretch to think you'd know that from the title.

DAY OF THE REFUGIOS
I was born in Nogales, Arizona,
On the border between
Mexico and the United States.

The places in between places
They are like little countries
Themselves, with their own holidays

Taken a little from everywhere.
My Fourth of July is from childhood,
Childhood itself a kind of country, too.

It's a place that's far from me now,
A place I'd like to visit again.
The Fourth of July takes me there.

In that childhood and border place
The Fourth of July, like everything else,
It meant more than just one thing.

In the United States the Fourth of July
It was the United States.
In Mexico it was the día de los Refugios,

The saint's day of people named Refugio.
I come from a family of people with names,
Real names, not-afraid names, with colors

Like the fireworks: Refugio,
Margarito, Matilde, Alvaro, Consuelo,
Humberto, Olga, Celina, Gilberto—

Names that take a moment to say,
Names you have to practice.
These were the names of saints, serious ones,

And so it was right to take a moment with them.
I guess that's what my family thought.
Our connection to saints was strong:

My grandmother's name—here it comes—
Her name was Refugio,
And my great-grandmother's name was Refugio,

And my mother-in-law's name now,
It's another Refugio, Refugios everywhere,
Refugios and shrimp cocktails and sodas.

Fourth of July was a birthday party
For all the women in my family
Going way back, a party

For everything Mexico, where they came from,
For the other words and the green
Tinted glasses my great-grandmother wore.

These women were me,
What I was before me,
So that birthday fireworks in the evening,

All for them,
This seemed right.
In that way the fireworks were for me, too.

Still, we were in the United States now,
And the Fourth of July,
Well, it was the Fourth of July.

But just what that meant,
In this border place and time,
It was a matter of opinion in my family.

This poem reminds me of my Christmases as well, and of the stories my father told me of growing up in the jungle.

"We didn't have Christmas on December 25," he would always say on December 25. "No. Our Christmas was on January 6, the '*Día de los Reyes Magos*,' or day of the wise kings."

Then he would always tell the story of the baseball bat, a present he received from his grandmother in the United States sometime in the early 1930s. It was a beautiful bat, he said, except that he didn't know what baseball was there in the jungle, where life revolved more around basic concerns, like gathering food and making the world work right. My father would always talk about what constituted food in the tropics of Tapachula—coconuts, sea turtles, iguanas, things that are hard to pick up, at least in any grocery store I've ever seen.

So there my father stood, not knowing about baseball, but he knew what he was holding anyway. He knew what this bat was in his life.

The bat was a perfect iguana killer.

That's what it became for him, and for my family as well, since we heard the story so many times.

January 6 is often also called Old Christmas. I once read in an anthropologist's report from 1940 about a small, Spanish-speaking town in New Mexico, Santo Domingo. The anthropologist was witnessing the Christmas festivities of January 6 and apparently did not understand Spanish all that well. So, rather than seeing that there was a *posada* procession in progress, where people carrying a Christ child go to different houses looking for shelter and, by ritual, are denied, the anthropologist got confused.

Trying to make sense of what he knew was called the *Día de los Reyes*, the word *reyes* meaning "kings," he reported that on this holiday the homes of people having the name of Reyes were being visited, though curiously not entered. He thought the holiday was for these people, which is funny in and of itself, but not altogether wrong.

My father would always go on to finish his baseball-bat story with how he got to visit his grandmother the next year in Nogales, and how it was his first time out of the tropics. He experienced snow for the first time, and almost died of fright. But what he did afterward was to ask for a postcard his grandmother had of a New England snow-covered scene. He took this back with him to show his friends in southern Mexico.

Aside from almost dying at the thought of the sky falling, he also learned something that he was to use to his advantage. Snow in Spanish is called *nieve*, which is also the Spanish word for ice cream. On getting back, he pulled out his postcard and showed all his friends.

"Yup," he told them. "Ice cream. Right out of the sky. Vanilla. See for yourself." After a few months, the vanilla became chocolate, and then strawberry.

My grandmother used to tell me a story about the day my father was born, how the volcano Tacaná erupted a few miles down from the house in which the family was living, a house with large windows in the tropics, at the southernmost tip of Mexico. She told me that what she remembers most from that day is how loud it was, how so many different animals came into the house, and how they tore through the mosquito nettings. The birds, especially, a great many tens of birds, came in and sat themselves up in the rafters to escape the ash and debris. The noise they made became, in her mind, as she told me many times, the noise my father made as he was being born.

It took me a long time to find myself in this story of my father's birthday, and yet I was there, in a story my parents were always telling me about my own birth. It concerns *el dieciséis de septiembre,* or the Sixteenth of September, celebrated as Mexico's independence from Spain.

Although I wasn't born until the early hours of September 18, my mother went into the hospital a week before. The old St. Joseph's Hospital was one block from the border. All my mother can remember of my being born, she says, is all the noise, all the music and singing and shouting.

This day, then, was my father's story, and my mother's story, and now my story as well. It was the right way to be born. The confusion of moment was now in me, too.

Tied to this particular story is the traditional *grito de dolores*, literally translated as "shout of pains," but meaning something more like "cry to arms," which starts the Sixteenth of September celebrations all over Mexico. It occurs late the night before, toward midnight, and recollects the historic day the humble priest Padre Hidalgo led the cry for freedom that spurred the Mexican Revolution.

It's either that or a commemoration in honor of my mother shouting as she was in labor.

Curiously enough from my perspective, *The Farmer's Almanac* reports that the sixteenth of September is also the day the Mayflower set sail from England.

Mexico's other independence day—it has two—is the Fifth of May, perhaps the most readily recognizable Mexican holiday in this country. It is the anniversary of the 1862 battle of Puebla, in which Mexican forces against overwhelming odds defeated French invaders.

On the Fifth of May, 1962, the border was opened, as it always was on this holiday, and the parade went from Nogales, Sonora, to Nogales, Arizona, with everyone mingling in between. Nobody worried about what that meant, or whether or not everyone would go home that night when the border gates were closed. Nobody worried because there was no need to worry. An open border meant just that. It didn't lead to panic or guns. It led to a good day.

But this didn't last.

The next year, John Kennedy was shot, and at the moment we got the news, I was a fifth-grader outside on the playground with some other kids watching, of all things, a millipede. It was a curious moment, possibly a metaphor for the greater event if

I wanted to work at it. But I've heard even Freud said that sometimes a cigar is just a cigar, so maybe the millipede was just a millipede, even if it had all those legs and scared us to death because we'd never seen anything like that before.

The news of course was devastating, and my teacher was crying. Saying what happened that day is vaguely regular, as I've heard so many people describe the day in much the same manner. But it's what happened later that shaped my greater memory of the day.

I was in a bowling league of all things, something concocted by the town, I think, to keep kids from getting into trouble. Bowling was on Fridays, and this was a Friday, so we went. The president had been shot, but nobody gave us further instruction. So we did what we did on every Friday: We went bowling.

What was not publicly announced was that on the day Kennedy was shot all the borders to this country were immediately closed. This is good on a national level. This makes sense.

But I was in this bowling league with a good number of friends who came from across the line. We got the phone call that the border had been closed, and that absolutely nobody was being allowed to cross—not parents, not children, not anybody. Who knew what disguise the assassin had used.

We all stood there in the echo chamber of the bowling alley, feeling the announcement reverberate. Bowling alleys have that thunderous capacity to make even silly announcements have authority. But today, rather than too much noise, it was not enough. I remember somebody starting to cry. Crying is by itself already something, but in a bowling alley, with its echo chamber, this is really something.

My memory of that day is of hearing stories of parents and children at the border just waiting into the night. Somebody at some point let them all through, but I picture this scene with parents and children and a fence between them, juxtaposed with the pictures of a dead president. I've asked my parents in later years about this, and that's what they remember too.

In traveling through Mexico after this, one of my most palpable memories is of seeing the small altars, called *ofrendas*, that various family members had in their houses, in San Luís Potosí and in Mexico City, where we had family. Far as these places were into Mexico, I saw that on each of these altars, among the renderings of saints, the *milagros*, and the photographs of family members going back a hundred years, there was a picture of John Kennedy.

I don't know what this means, but even then I knew it meant something, and it's lasted. Thinking of his picture on those altars still gives me goose bumps. The day Kennedy was shot is not a holiday exactly. It's something more: a bittersweet consideration, a day meant to remember, rather than perhaps to celebrate. There are others.

My father-in-law used to tell a story of the *Día de San Francisco Xavier*, or the feast of St. Francis Xavier, the patron saint of the Tohono O'odham and of the town of Magdalena, Sonora. Starting late in September, for two weeks, I remember seeing hundreds and possibly thousands of native Indians, Mexicans, and Arizona residents as they walked, along the river and along the road, the sixty-five miles from Nogales to Magdalena. It was a show of penance or devotion, and timed so that they would all arrive there on October 4, the feast of San Francisco. Some people would walk the entire distance on their knees, depending on their *manda*, or promise, to the saint.

When my father-in-law was a young man, he went on one of these walks with his grandmother, who was ill at the time and could not walk. So what he did was to carry their bags—which were considerable as this was a week-long walk at least—he carried their bags ahead a mile, and set them down. Then he came back for his grandmother and carried her piggyback two miles ahead. Then he walked back a mile, got the bags, and ran them ahead two miles, a mile past his grandmother, coming back, and so on.

These walks, and all the things like them, were from the days when people had a stake in things. When you were born mattered, and what you celebrated on what day came down from the decades and the centuries. Maybe not always clearly, but that's where it came from. And one had better pay attention.

I come from a large extended family, and there were some relatives I only saw on holidays, and for me that's what named them. Not only might you know what food you were going to eat on a particular day, but you also knew who you were going to see. That was as much a part of the ritual as anything else. Who you saw when, and what they did.

This is sometimes a confusion in itself, a confusion of feeling in what should be sure. On all the Christmases I can remember, one or another of my many uncles, for example, just like one of yours, by the time he got to anybody's house would have already been celebrating for some time, celebrating Old Christmas, new Christmas, and anything else that lit itself up like he did. It's like he and the holiday were buddies:

UNCLE CHRISTMAS
Not more vulgar than any other
Uncle, he knew his place
Among them, but he was the most

Uncle of the uncles,
And when he died
He did it well, filled

With the resonant
Earth-rich failings of his kidneys,
Whiskey and his big life,

Summed up in the same space
His stomach took,
That kindly thing

Which had kept his belt buckle
From harm, which had kept him
From hugging his nieces

The way he wanted.
It hung there,
A cement mixer, mixing

A concrete we could hear inside.
No shirt was adequate.
His one suit coat fit

Like sideburns on a face.
Everything I knew about him
Was stomach,

His hungover days
Pouring gravel
With the highway department

Dressed in hard colored vests
Orange and yellow
As if they were hunters.

These were the fabled
Men who made noise
At women.

He was called "the goat,"
But it was friendly.
No one told us why.

He had a thin moustache
The kind from the movies,
Red skin, black hair

And delicate hands.
The beer went straight to his eyes,
Which were always angel fish

In the back room of a pet shop,
The way you look at them
Moving at soft angles

Through the glass.
I remember his yard and the dog,
His perfect sons

He loved more than his wife.
They could have anything,
And even as a child I understood

This extreme unction at work,
This long dying.
Christ of the beers,

His lesson in how to be the man.
He suffered himself
And was happy.

❀

I sometimes don't know what other people's holidays are now, but I've still got one more of my own. Thanksgiving. Not the one that's in the books though—Thanksgiving in my house had nothing to do with the Pilgrims.

My parents are both from somewhere else, which makes me a first-generation American. The Pilgrims in that sense are mine, I suppose. But my parents think about the day in other terms.

I can think of my mother crying on only two occasions, both of which come to me as stories. When my mother came to this country from England, from having lived through the Battle of Britain, through the War itself, and having trained as a nurse, my father, just after they were married in Nogales, took her to the grocery store.

They walked into the Veterans' Market and my mother's eyes were wide, but she played it cool.

"How much can we get," she asked my father.

"What do you mean?" he asked. "You can get as much as you want. Whatever you want."

My mother, who could not remember having lived in Britain without rationing, just stood there and cried. There's a holiday in that, I think.

Later that first year in their marriage, my mother, knowing that my father liked pecan pies, baked one for him on Thanksgiving. It became a tradition after that, and one pie became two, and then ten, and then twenty, until in their heyday a few years ago my parents were making forty to fifty pies on Thanksgiving, for family, for friends, for the entire town. It's my absolute association with the holiday—eating my parents' pecan pies, which they always made together on one very, very busy Sunday the weekend before the holiday. Those pecan pies are legendary. "It's the rum," my parents would always say.

I recently asked my mother about them.

"I didn't know the English made pecan pies," I said off-handedly, assuming all these years that she had brought the recipe with her, and that perhaps it had been a family secret handed down—who knew—for maybe hundreds of years.

"They don't," she said. "The English don't make pecan pies."

"Then how did you start making all these pies?" I asked.

"Oh," she said, "the recipe was on the back of a bottle of Karo syrup."

But the story wasn't really over. In that first pie my mother made to please my father, that first year, she put a cup of salt into the recipe instead of a cup of sugar, so that when my father tasted it his face just dropped. My mother—this was the second time—burst into tears. And so my father took her into the kitchen, and together they made a second pie, their first of many together.

That's Thanksgiving.

These pecan pies—their smell of brown sugar and hot rum in the air—lead me to food, and perhaps something stronger in defining holidays.

We often remember holidays not so much because of the event they commemorate, but because of the food we associate with them. We can say all we want on holidays, make speeches and have parades, but when do we eat? And the thing is, we know what's coming. We know what the food will be. The holiday in this way is ordered not so much by the calendar as by the stove. We remember holidays because we remember what we ate on them. The food itself became a vocabulary to use and enjoy. It became its own language.

❁

I think all of this leads us to the Day of the Dead, which are really the days of the various dead. By now, after a great deal of various media attention, people probably don't need much more explanation of the holiday—the skeletons in funny poses on all sorts of things seems to be enough.

This is all wonderful. It gets a great deal of press, and I like it. But what we've seen in the news or in books or in newspapers, of course, gathers all the small observations together into one mega-day. It's a good festival and a good way to keep the day, but I don't actually know anybody who did all these things. And, in fact, much about these festivities comes in little bits from farther south in Mexico and from all over Latin America. This was not as big an event in Sonora, at least until people started migrating up from farther south.

To tell the truth, Day of the Dead for my family in Nogales, growing up in the Fifties and Sixties, mostly meant that someone in the family was put in charge of going to the cemetery and cleaning the family graves. Somebody would go, but not everybody. It was an earnest responsibility, and the rest of the family felt better getting the phone call that said everything had been taken care of, and that, yes, the graves all had fresh flowers, daisies and chrysanthemums—not marigolds, which stink, even though marigolds, *cempasúchiles*, are the traditional flower of the dead, but so what, and yes, the mud on the headstones from the last rain was all cleaned off. It was like that.

We knew about the other things that happened on Day of the Dead, but we didn't do much about them. We had all seen the candy skulls and maybe tasted the *pan de muertos*, the bread of the dead, and all the rest. But for us the day was simply quieter, more personal and more family. Besides, things like Halloween were taking over, which required a more immediate attention. The dead have a patient streak a mile long, but kids wanting their costumes fixed do not. And so, slowly, the day became generous in its quietude. It let the living do what they do best.

In this way, the Day of the Dead began to be blended with Halloween, and it was an enamored sharing that continues today, especially at the border.

It's a crude, capillary action: There is exchange, a borrowing, one holiday for another, but it is rough and curious. It is candy for candy, but in different wrappers, from homemade skulls in napkins to cellophane-wrapped candy bars. In fact, I came across a bag of candies made by Brach's called "Neckbone Nick," and it's full of candy skulls and ribs and femurs.

The day of the dead, in truth, means not just all dead, but the day of our dead, and more personally, the day of my dead. I remember the lives inside my life. It is all of us remembering ourselves, underscoring that even a single life is within itself a complex community. And that's where holidays ultimately reside—inside.

The Day of the Dead, even though it's better known now than ever, it's a hard sell in this century of progress. If holidays in general are difficult to sort out, then this one is particularly so, and especially in this country. Nobody wants to talk about death. Somebody said that what Americans really want are tragedies with happy endings.

But the tradition and the day, all of it comes down to something simple: to understanding one part of what it means to be human. The Day of the Dead is, in fact, a day of sadness. But it is not a day of regret.

I think we're all at work sorting our calendars out. What it is, is that sometimes as human beings we just simply feel something. That feeling has value. That's what holidays are. That's what this day and the others like it are about.

These days, my own holidays, my own anniversaries, may be unfocused on the calendar, but they are fine-tuned in the heart. If you say Thanksgiving to me, I know what I will think.

CAPIROTADA

Last week I asked my mother-in-law, Refugio Barron, a question about something my grandmother, who was also named Refugio, and whose mother, my great-grandmother, was also named Refugio, used to make, something I had eaten often as a child—*capirotada*. Maybe "eaten" isn't quite the right word—I used to pick at it while everybody laughed. But picking at it was the right way to go. There was gold and rock both in this dish.

Menudo and *tamales* and *buñuelos* belong to Christmas and New Year's, and there are other foods for other times. But my favorite, not because I liked the taste of it but because of its P. T. Barnum scale of production, was always *capirotada*, and always at Lent—at Lent because as a bread pudding it had no meat.

Capirotada: This is indeed simply a bread pudding, but it would be unfair to stop there in the description. "Bread pudding" says so little about it, as so many words are unequal to their task. Made with a zoo of foods, each thing in it is good, but taken together *Capirotada* is Mexican cooking's version of fruitcake, but raised several notches to the level of a one-ring circus, with everybody and everything gathered at the grand finale. It assembles into the single ring at the center, and in view of the full spotlight, all the star performers, the high-wire walkers, the elephants and clowns, beasts from the far ends of the cooking cosmos: prunes and peanuts, white bread, raisins, milk, *quesadilla* cheese, butter, cinnamon and cloves, old world sugar. All this, and those things people will not tell you.

But telling and talking about making it, buying all the ingredients, and so on—this was fun. Everything in it was precious, almost jewel-like in its discussion and placement in the recipe, but actually eating the thing itself was another story altogether.

I am reminded of *capirotada* in the story of the medieval pope who was given ground diamonds as a cure for stomach problems. The idea at the time was that if diamonds were valuable and God's most precious expression, then a diet of them for the pope made divine sense. But the roughly crushed diamonds, of course, completely ground up the pope's insides.

Still, the nature of this food is in keeping with the extremity of Lent. *Capirotada* looks garish at first, so much food, all together, without a break or a breath. But the excess is the point: It's the far side of good. If each thing is good, then the whole cannot be wrong. But of course that's the kind of thinking that kills popes.

Well, *capirotada* was revolting. But the stories, the whole process of making *capirotada*, this was pure elegance in all the rules that had to be followed. The ingredients for *capirotada* had to be gathered from across the line, in Nogales, Sonora, or else certainly from Mexico—and this is one of the things that defined its making. It was not from here.

The peanuts had to be raw, the *panocha* sugar had to be unrefined and coarse, the cheese had to be just the right farmer cheese. And in Mexico, you didn't buy these ingredients by any label that fit neatly on a package. You bought them instead by description and by narrative: "Please give me two kilos of cheese, for *capirotada*." That got you a nod of the head and the right cheese, and was completely different from simply naming the ingredient. You didn't just buy a food—you earned it. You had to know its story. This was a test.

❀

"You make it with white bread, *panocha*, raisins, prunes, peanuts, white *quesadilla* cheese, butter, cinnamon, and cloves.

"The white bread can be any kind. If it's a whole loaf, you cut it up, but if it's already cut, that's perfect. The *panocha*, that's like sugarloaf, the shape like a cone, but this is unrefined, and a deep brown inside. People in other places call it *piloncillo*, but not here. You know, it's *panocha*. Very thick."

I nodded my head to say that *yes*, I understood. It was all I could do.

"The cheese," my mother-in-law continued, keeping a stride that could not now be broken, "it's got to be the creamy kind, *quesadilla*, white cheese with lots of cream so that it's runny. Farmers' cheese. Like in Imuris. They make this cheese only homemade, on cloth towels. Always in a round shape, *panela*, round and about two inches thick. Not the dry kind of white cheese, the kind that crumbles. That's for other dishes.

"The rest of the things—it's wherever you get them.

"You make a honey with the cinnamon and cloves. You add some water, *panocha*, the cinnamon, and the cloves. You boil them together on the stove until it turns into a honey, and then put it aside. But keep it warm. It'll stay warm anyway, don't worry. But don't forget, either.

"Gather the cheese, the peanuts, the raisins, and the prunes. Get the bread, cut it up if you need to, toast it, and put butter on all sides. How much bread you use depends on how far you want the *capirotada* to go.

"Get a pan, and grease it with butter.

"Put a layer of the bread at the bottom of the pan, making sure this first layer of bread is especially buttered on the bottom.

"Put down a layer of the other ingredients, one by one, raisins, prunes, peanuts, cheese—a lot of cheese. Drizzle each layer with the honey. Honey each time, until you reach the top of the pan.

"Don't move the bread for any reason, or the concoction will mix into itself and become a mess.

"At the end, top the mixture with cheese, a great deal of cheese.

"Cover the pan. Expect that it will be a moist mixture. Put on a light fire, a low heat, however you cook. After about twenty minutes to half an hour, the honey will bubble, and it will cook all the other ingredients.

"Cook further for about thirty minutes to forty-five minutes. It's done because the bread will be moist, the cheese will be melted, and the peanuts will change taste—they'll taste like peanuts, but different.

"Once done, the top of the *capirotada* will still look moist. If you want, you can put it in the oven uncovered for a while to brown the top.

"It's a lot of work.

"This is a Sonoran *capirotada*. In the south, they add pineapple and banana. But this is a Sonoran dish, fixed this way, like *carne machaca* and *menudo* and flour *tortillas* and deer meat.

"And well, maybe you remember this, it's made during Lent, during *Cuaresma*, for just after. You put everything into it the same way you just gave up everything for a week. It's a food that helps you make up in one sitting for everything you couldn't have before. It's like a food piñata.

"And it's not just *capirotada* at this time of year. It's made along with *chicos*, crushed corn, a special corn, so that it has a little seedlike or grit quality. It doesn't sound too good, but it is. The Tarahumara make it, but you can buy it.

"And potato *tortillas*, made with a special *masa*—potato, corn *masa*, white cheese, and milk. You make a *torta*, a fat or thickly formed *tortilla*, of this and fry it in grease. Put cut-up fresh tomato, green chili, onion, and cilantro on top. And lettuce. And bake a fresh tomato and squeeze it to make a juice to put on top as well. You eat the *torta*, itself, as something. It doesn't have anything in it—it doesn't hold meat or chicken. *Tortas de papa*. They're just what they are, and worth the trouble.

❀

I left her at that point in the story, but I think she kept on talking. My being there or not being there had little to do with the magnificence of a recipe that's been around for centuries.

"That's how some things are," she said later when I came back after eating lunch, hardly having noticed my departure. "That's how they stay around, don't you think? They're trouble, everybody knows it. They're trouble and work and worry, but I can't ever say I'm sorry when it's all done."

GREEN CARDS

ALL COLORS EXIST TO SATISFY THE LONGING FOR BLUE.

There's a folk saying in Spanish, *el que quiera azul que le cueste*. One must pay for what one wants. It's a variation of the older Spanish proverb, "Take what you want and pay for it, says God." But the phrase means, more literally, *he who wants blue, let it cost him*.

A green card is what you get if you are a citizen of another country but you find yourself in, or cross over to, the United States. The card is a first step toward applying for citizenship. My wife, who was born in Mexico, had one. My mother, who was born in England, had one. My father, born in Mexico, didn't have one. But that's another story, involving some curious papers and shady explanations. My mother-in-law, after more than forty years here, still has one. She's never been quite sure what to do next. But she's learned well that you don't raise your hand to ask the Immigration Service anything. They notice you then. Everybody knows that.

They notice you and then they do something. And they're everywhere, maybe. So you don't speak loudly, you don't ask questions, you don't make trouble. Run away when you have to. Don't sign anything. Get a job only where everybody else is getting one, where it's safe.

There were all kinds of stories. The one my mother-in-law lived with the longest was how, her sister in Guaymas told her, they had heard that when you become a citizen of the United States you have to spit on the flag of Mexico. And they would all shake their heads in a *no*.

My mother, when she became a citizen, recalls a curious moment. After the ceremony, the high school band came into the courtroom and, because she was special—which is to say, in this border town with Mexico, she was not Mexican—they played the British national anthem. Someone thought it was a good idea. At that moment, though, she says she felt a little funny. She never forgot.

None of these stories is easy, and nobody knows what will happen when you cross over, and everybody is not treated the same.

❄

Crossing over from Mexico was more than just being there and then being here. It was a change in everything, a change even in how one walked, if only because to stand here is simply to stand in a different place, physically. In Mexico the ground moved one way, coiled and trailed and offered itself. Here was not there, and the coiling and trailing and offering were to the left and to the right but never the same. To this, the legs and the body had to adjust. It was not the same ground.

And it was a change in color. In Mexico the color my family remembers most was green—they had lived in the jungle, after all, which was something all by itself, but there was also a green in the churches—the color of the Virgin of Guadalupe's clothes—and a green, a vivid green, in the Mexican flag, which flew everywhere but whose color was always somewhere in between vivid and faded, arriving at a shade that could not be reproduced, only lived. Leaving Mexico and coming to the United States, the eyes, like the legs, have to learn over.

Here the color is blue. Blue in all kinds of things, and with abandon. If one cannot find the Mexican greens here, the blues are a discovery. There is blue in Mexico, but not this blue. Not so much blue. It's in the new cars and in the stripes of a new flag, a different sky and a different light that seems to come down from that sky. That light enters people's eyes, and turns them blue as well.

If the eyes were new, there were smells that were also new, so the nose had to adapt itself as well. But after so many small changes regarding so many things, one began—if only slightly—to look different.

The body and the mirror made their changes.

❧

My father told me a very short but always very funny and very sad story about his grandfather on his mother's side, Alberto, who had blue eyes. He worked on the family ranch in Mexico during the week, but during the weekend he would go into town—probably Magdalena—and get drunk, passing out in the street. I don't know that anyone in the family would say it quite that way, or want to hear it, but that's what my father said.

The Indians that also came into town, or who lived there, and who must have been Yaqui or Mayo, knew him and would wait for him. When Saturday night became Sunday morning, and he had just found his rest wherever he happened to be, they would take turns going over to where he lay. One at a time and carefully, they would lift first one of his eyelids and then the other to look at the blue, which nobody had seen up close before. And to see it twice, this was worth the wait and the risk.

That's all there was to the story, but it was about blue, even then. It was sometimes so strange to have blue in Mexico, this momentary blue, that sometimes all one could do was stop and look at it.

❀

Crossing over from Mexico to the United States was a big step, but that part was easy. Big things are like that—easy to identify and, with a deep breath, done all at once. As life turned out, it was the small that was difficult. The small things—which is all the opposite of what one might think.

These smaller things begin with signing papers, but first with walking to the office to sign papers, and first before that with asking directions to the office: The day is filled not just with what needs to be done, but with all the things one forgets as well.

These details, and there are so many: This is the everything that makes a day—but a day unlike any before, to be followed by so many again, so many days without directions for all of what really needs to be done. This world of papers and buildings and uniforms and information is a place, a country unto itself, with its own rules and laws, its own way of doing things. Even time is different here. Some people move into this country-of-the-in-between, and live there all their lives. Some of my family, this is where I write to them. There are in return no postcards to show off this place.

❀

I remember something from the middle of all this, from the middle of color and the middle of the century. During the Fifties, I remember driving through town and seeing pickup trucks full of men dressed in white. They were *braceros*, the workers imported specifically from Mexico for a brief time, sometimes only a day, just to work. After work, either at the end of the day or the end of the growing season, they had to go back to Mexico. What that meant was taking the pickup truck to the border and dropping them all off.

Arizona was the last state to hold out against minimum wage, championing the *laissez faire* system of government oversight: In this case, let the growers pay what the workers will accept and don't get in the way. And these workers worked for almost nothing. It seemed, for a while, like a good idea to the growers and to the government, whose program this was.

As a kid, I remember only all these men dressed in white, and that they looked like nuns to me then. I didn't know why they dressed like that. But I did know, even then, as I watched pickup trucks full of them driving through town, it was a color that meant they didn't belong anywhere.

※

For my family, crossing over was crossing over from green, not from Mexico. Nobody left Mexico. I don't think Crossing Over was so large, with such capital letters, or so absolute. It was more gradual, one aunt at a time, one more cousin, and always with somebody deciding not to cross over, so there were tears, too. People crossed over with tears as one more suitcase to carry.

If much of my family crossed over from green, then, instead of Mexico, it was to travel into blue—not the United States. Again, it was not the big names that served people.

Blue was the far other side of the green on this map of the heart, existing perhaps somewhere in imagination only. And of course, no place is one color. Green did not disappear on coming to this country, and Mexico had—and still has—its own magnificent shades of blue. If one changed in coming across the border, one also remained the same. But the changes got all the attention, as changes will.

After the circus of it all, however, after blinking at the neon of the new, there was indeed something difficult to describe here, though it was desperately quiet so as not to attract attention. Whatever the new was, it was what it had always been: It was you yourself. In new clothes, looking different, smelling different: But it was you.

In this way the green stayed, as the center, as the life we would return to upon waking from this dream of a new place. The green lurks even now in the way the Virgin of Guadalupe is still painted—we had found her again! She was here, too, waiting for us. And green in the shades of the hillside houses just across the border at Nogales. It has stayed in the Chinese teas my family has drunk, in the *yerba buena*, how that green herb was a cure for things, and in the afternoons, in talk.

Green stayed, finally. It had a place in my family, sometimes only as a memory, but always as something that happened, as everything that happened. It stayed as a sadness for something.

It stayed as what used to be.

THE SAME HOUSE

When I was a few years old, my parents had a plan for going to the movies. They didn't have a car, or enough money for a babysitter, so what they would do was simple and to the point. My mother would walk down to the early show, watch it, then run back after it was finished. My father would run as fast as he could to make the second showing, each taking a turn babysitting me. When my father got back, then they'd talk about the movie. It was early time management, or time shifting. They were ahead of their decade, though I don't think they were particularly happy about it.

I've always wondered if they saw the same movie, despite the apparent circumstances. They sat, after all, in different seats, went at different times, sat next to different people. Who knows? But even a small difference must carry some weight. In the midst of apparent familiarity, on some level they remained strangers.

My father died in the fall, and I think of this story now more than ever. The house I grew up in always had him in it. Now that I go there, it's the same house, and my mother is there, and I've touched everything inside hundreds of times. I know it's easy to say that his presence was part of that house, and that his absence now is what changes things—there's not much epiphany in that. But it's what my body feels that surprises me, the something physical that I feel in that house. I don't know if I feel more or if I feel less, I simply feel different.

What this adds up to is nothing new, but that doesn't mean we've come to any useful understanding of it—we might share the strength of the feeling, but that's all. The science of sorrow: We have not harnessed this power, only felt it, and for centuries.

I say it is a thing, and not simply a feeling. We err in that we do not contain it and let it take its rightful place alongside electricity in lighting up our houses.

My parents, in going to the same movie—in the same movie house, in the same town, on the same day—but at different times, built into themselves and into me something, however slight, about perspective. As I get older, and as people leave me, I am trying to shepherd not simply what I know, but what I feel as well. I want it all to have value and purpose. When the familiar changes, I want the lights to go on, the water to flow, and gas to feed into the stove. I want it to count. We all do. We all feel that power.

I hand this moment to the scientists.

FROM NOGALES TO NOGALES

In 1946, when he was fourteen, my father took a deep breath and ran away from home. But his family was so large, it was only his home he was running away from. His family was everywhere. When he came to Nogales, Arizona, of course it was to stay with his aunts and his grandmother. He went to high school for a year there, and then tried to join the Army.

He passed the physical and joined the Army and went to boot camp. But he had not come across the border from Mexico legally. Just coming across and going to high school and having aunts and a grandmother here weren't enough. He had to have papers. When the Army found that there were no papers, they kicked him out. My father told me several accounts of this time, and they were all different. I'm not sure he ever told anybody what really happened, not even my mother.

The story he told me, quietly one day when it was just the two of us, is that he was ingloriously discharged and deported back to Mexico. He laughed and said all this meant, really, is that they took him in a truck and dropped him off at the border and told him to get lost.

And he did get lost, in his own way. He came back across the border, applied once more, and went through the whole routine again—only this time, he switched his name around to Alberto Alvaro. This was before computers or anything like that, and paperwork took awhile to catch up with people. Anyway, he said, Alberto was easier for people to pronounce here.

And difficulty in pronouncing words must have been important to him, since he didn't yet know very much English. Still, joining up must have been what he wanted. He had heard that if you came from another country and joined the armed services and completed a full tour of duty, you got U.S. citizenship. At least, that's how it was during WW II. He hoped it would still work.

I think the real story is that he had crossed over on a student visa, but had really come to find a job. I know he worked at a grocery story, appropriately called *La Frontera*, which means "the border." But either way, he was accepted, again, by the Army, went through boot camp again, and got assigned.

There was still plenty to do in the world, apparently, in the aftermath of the war and with the ripening of the Korean conflict. My father went to France, to North Africa, and to England, where he was stationed in my mother's hometown of Warrington. During this time he was decorated for participating in the Berlin airlift, as a paratrooping medic. I can't imagine my father jumping out of an airplane, but he did it more than fifty times. The Army by this time had split up, into the Army and the Army Air Force, and he chose to go with the Air Force for most of his tour of duty. Since he was in the air so much, I guess it made sense.

He was a staff sergeant by this time, had taught himself English, and had finished a high school degree. The intricacies of his first enlistment's paperwork, however, caught up with him again, but apparently it didn't amount to much. I imagine he was thankful, because he was still scared, but he shouldn't have been.

My father had signed up for a regular tour of duty, three years, in 1947, but his service ended up lasting four. He was caught by what was called the "Truman year," in which President Truman, given the volatile state of the world, simply declared that anyone who was in the service would serve an extra year. My father would get U.S. citizenship, but we all read later how they put those troops trying to become citizens, and those with African-Americans, all in the line of fire.

It had been a rocky start for my father in the service, and it was a rocky end. My father had started his tour of duty at Lackland Air Force Base in Texas, and he didn't have a very good time. The service itself was good to him, but Texas was less hospitable. My father had very dark skin, and difficulty with English in those days. He ran into signs he would never forget, and was always telling me about Texas. "No Dogs or Mexicans," he said. He saw it more than once.

It made me scared to go to Texas, to be honest. And I think he was telling me for my own good, given the only experience he had. I've since been to Texas many times, however, and I told him whenever he asked or was concerned that things had changed, at least in my experience. He would shake his head and tell me I should just be careful.

❀

The end of his service was no easier. The lucky part, however, was that he was stationed in my mother's hometown, and that's how they came to meet. He was a medic, and my mother was a nurse, working at the Royal Warrington Infirmary. There were parties. It was cold. I don't want to know anymore.

It just happened. They got engaged, and my mother's family always treated him very well. Even though he was very dark, something my father thought about a lot, and my mother very light, the specter of whatever might have been raised never was. They simply didn't see it.

On a dinner visit one night, my mother and my father both told this story of my father sitting down with the family to eat. They were having steak, which they offered him. My father said thank you very much, and without thinking he took the one steak on the platter. The others ate what was on their plates, and the evening went very well. What my mother told my father later was that steak was severely rationed, and the single steak he took was their only meat for the month. It was meant for all of them, but my father didn't know. It was a big night for everyone.

But things went well and my father learned, as he had been doing all along. My parents were to be married just as soon as he was discharged. They would live in Warrington, and had already found a rental, which was one of the requirements for my father staying in England. They had to have evidence of domicile and some other things, but this was the most important. My mother ordered her wedding gown, and the wedding cake. My parents, who were both Catholic, had the banns read at my mother's lifelong church, St. Benedict's, where she had also gone to school. Everything was in order.

However, my father's commanding officer did not feel the same way about my father, apparently, as my mother and her family—and the English in general—did. Whether this was unspoken Air Force policy, or whether it was his CO's own idea, I don't know. And neither do my parents. But two weeks before my father was to be discharged, the CO shipped my father back to the States. This was clearly so that the marriage would not happen.

Everything my father worried about came into play in this moment. He had only enough time to go to my mother's house, give her some money, tell her he loved her, and that he would be waiting for her in Salt Lake City. And then he left.

My mother had been no farther than Blackpool in her entire life. Blackpool was two train stops away from Warrington, on the shore. Two train stops.

I can only imagine that she took a breath, which she would need for what she did next. She packed her bags, said goodbye to her friends, said goodbye to her parents and her sister and her brother, and she got on an ocean liner bound for the United States. All she had was my father's voice saying he would meet her.

My mother would not return for twenty-seven years. Her brother, whom she always called "Our Joe," as the English do, was seven when she left, and it was the only way she could remember him in all those years. In all my mother's stories, her family stayed young. When she went back, he was in his middle thirties, married, and with a daughter of his own.

My mother got on a boat, crossed the ocean, crossed the country, and got off the train at Salt Lake City. And there was my father.

❀

When I came across from England it was on the Medea. I still have all the things they handed out on that boat, but you've seen them. We got just so far from New York though, a mile or something, and we all had to line up because they wanted to see everybody's papers. You had to have had chest X-rays and blood work.

There was something of mine that was missing or that had been misplaced. I didn't know if they were going to let me in, and I worried myself sick. I sent a telegram to your father asking if couldn't he please meet me in New York. He telegrammed back saying that he couldn't, please be brave. They finally said it was okay. And we found the papers later anyway. I think they just thought I was all right.

There was this couple, the Brooks, who could tell I was scared, and they took me under their wing that first night in New York. I had never been anywhere, and I didn't know what to do. We had to stay in New York overnight, and the Brooks took care of me. We stayed in the Hotel New Yorker, and the next morning I got on a train to Salt Lake City.

But there was a layover in Chicago, three hours. I had said goodbye to the Brooks, and so I was all by myself and really didn't know what to do. The train people told me which station I would have to go to so I could catch my train, and I went there and didn't move. I was hungry and had money, but I didn't move, I was so scared. I just waited there the whole time and didn't even look around until I got on the train and went to Salt Lake City.

When I got off the train, you know I didn't see your father and didn't see him. It turns out we were at opposite ends of the train, and so it took a long time to find him. He had a guy with him that he had met and they were both looking for me. I finally saw him, just when I didn't know what I was going to do.

They took me to the hotel they were staying at. They must have told my story to everybody. The manager sent a great big bowl of fruit to my room, I'll never forget, since I hadn't had fruit in years because of rationing.

Your father took me to the show that night. It was about a cat that was left millions of dollars. It was called "Rhubarb." He took me shopping, and bought me a pair of snakeskin shoes. I don't know why, but maybe you remember seeing them. I kept them a long time.

The following day, we got on the bus, which we were going to take from Salt Lake City to Nogales. We had to change busses a few times, and when we were coming to the last legs of the trip, there were big open stretches of land. There was a cloud of dust I saw, a dust devil, and your father said that it was Indians coming to chase the bus. I believed him.

Then when we got to Tucson, the bus was full, but they found room for us. The bus was full of Indians, which I didn't know. They didn't look like Indians in the movies. They were all going to Nogales, where they would then walk to Magdalena to make their pilgrimages in honor of Saint Francis. It was very big in those days.

❀

Your father's family was all in Nogales, now, since his father died, your grandfather, just before your father joined the service. But your grandfather, Margarito, he's a whole other story. I never met him. Your grandmother, though, and her mother, your great-grandmother, and everybody, they were all very nice to me. I stayed with them before the wedding. But it was hard because they didn't speak any English and I didn't speak any Spanish yet.

There was a funny thing that happened. When we got married, the altar boy gave me a prayer book in Spanish, which I couldn't recognize, so I just had to pretend. But I did it okay. I remember that the altar boy had a cold and sniffled the whole time.

I walked down the aisle with a borrowed veil, Mary Lou's, which we didn't have time to try on beforehand. César, your father's brother, was the best man, and I said to him the whole time my veil is going to fall off. It was so big and so long, bigger and longer than I was.

But going back down the aisle I was braver because I was married. I just pulled it up myself and didn't worry about it at all.

It was 1951, that year we got married. At first, your father didn't have a job and we didn't have any money. He went out looking for a job and went over to Mr. Don Dan's Texaco station.

He hired your father, and Missy, and Chapo. He worked there for only seven or eight months, but he never forgot that this man gave him his first job. Your father got thirty dollars a week at Don Dan's, and had to try selling Electrolux vacuum cleaners as well. We got one at a discount, and kept it, I don't know, thirty years. You remember it, and the gray box it came in.

I didn't have any new clothes in the first five years we were married, just what I brought with me from England. But things were all right. We used to go to the Obregón Theater across the line, always to watch the Mexican actor Cantinflas. I didn't understand the language, but the things he did made me laugh.

The very first Cinco de Mayo that I was here I got caught by something famous they used to do across the line. It was a papier maché bull full of lit firecrackers, and they used to run into the crowd with it. I was hopping and hopping but one of the firecrackers got me and burned me on the leg. It burned through my dress and my slip. Your father kept saying, stay still, stay still, and nothing will happen to you. Well, the one that got me hurt, but it wasn't enough to leave a scar.

❦

The very first dinner I cooked for your father was roast beef, potatoes, green beans, and salad. We bought it all at Puchi's Downtown Grocery Story.

In England we ate a lot of meat and potato pies, and French fries on the side. It's all we had. And rabbit pie. You buy the rabbit frozen and then put so much water with a little salt on to boil. Cut the rabbit into pieces and boil for an hour. Add vegetables and let that cook for another half-hour. Put a pastry on top, and let it brown. You had this when you were little, but I don't think you remember.

Your father, he liked the pastry things. I used to make hot pot that way, too. It's meat that's cooked in the oven and then afterward you add onions and potatoes and gravy browning for color. The vegetables cook in with the meat. I would make pastry, about an inch thick, and lay it over the top of the dish and let it brown.

It was easy to move from this to hot dogs, even though these were new for me. But the bread was like a pastry, a little. And hamburgers, too—though I'd had them, but from the base in England where your father used to get them.

You know, I used to put butter on the bread and then scrape it all off. You got to eat whatever stayed on. I did this because I couldn't get used to things not being rationed. I think that's why I started making so many things. I made a rhubarb pie once, like they had in England. It was canned. Rice puddings with milk and sugar. Custards. Mince pies. Tarts, mince and jam tarts. Of course, all of this was made out of jars. They were great.

This was my first year.

But coming from England to here, and being married now, I started making things that your father liked. I learned to make tortillas. It was day by day, and I wasn't in England. There was just one rule, though: Every meal here had beans, no matter what.

I guess there were other rules, but it took longer to figure them out. The first year I was here I didn't know what Thanksgiving was, and I didn't know the whole family went to Belita's, your great-grandmother's. I said no, that we weren't going to go because your father always worked on Thursdays and I always fixed lunch. I just didn't realize what an important day Thanksgiving was.

They came over to the house and asked me again, but I still said I didn't think we were going to make it. Well then they sent Aunt Matilde over to the house—you know what that means—and she said we better get over there. She talked in Spanish to your father, saying Belita was the head of the family and we better go. I just didn't know. The whole family was there, and everybody who was even just barely family. I just didn't know. I just thought it was an invitation to lunch.

It seems a little strange, now, to remember that and to think how it's such an American holiday. Things were confusing.

For example, during Lent your grandmother used to make the best capirotada, and she gave some to everyone in the family. Every Friday. Looking at it, I used to think capirotada was a meal, and I would give it to your father for lunch on Fridays. Just capirotada and nothing else. He never said a word, and just ate it. But it was really just a bread pudding.

I started to learn to make everything. Your father was a great cook himself, and he was the one who taught me how to make everything. He just didn't have the time to always do it himself. The way he learned was, he had just paid attention. He told me he used to cook pigeon breasts for his mother when he was little.

And I made a lot of carne machaca—we used to buy regular meat, the kind for cheap steaks, and hang it on the clothesline and make sure the dogs weren't around. We'd cover it with old bedsheets to keep the flies off, dry it for a couple of days, then bring it in and smash it up with a hammer. Then you would fry onions and tomatoes in some oil, add the carne machaca, and let it cook. Sometimes we'd try to dry it inside. And you had to bring the meat in at night.

There was that, then, and menudo, which the first time I tasted it I thought I was going to die. It's the same as tripe in England, but it's steamed over there and served with salt and vinegar and served cold. Having it warm was yuk. Stop laughing.

It reminds me of the first time I made tripas, which are intestines. I got them the day before, and I was going to make them for lunch the next day. I washed them really well, but noticed a bunch of gook inside them. I turned them inside out and washed them really well there, too. I ended up serving your father simply intestine skin. As it turns out, the gook is what has all the flavor.

❧

We lived those first years on the second story of a four-apartment building on Rodriguez Street, right behind the Catholic church. It wasn't much. But from the porch we could hear the whole town. We could hear the high school football game, and always knew if the Apaches were winning or losing. That was important because the movies and the football game were only a quarter, but we didn't have enough to go to both. We could hear the church bells, of course. They always rang when somebody died. And at twelve o'clock every day. On Sunday it was all day for the masses.

We could see a lot from there, too. I could see right down into the church grounds, and where the priests lived. I could see the high school, and all the houses below us, and all the way down Rodriguez Street. I could always see you walking all the way down to Mrs. Barker's house. We could see the hills of across the line and all the colorful houses all over them.

You were born in the old hospital, St. Joseph's, right on the line. They used to celebrate in those days for a whole week before and a whole week afterward the dieciséis de septiembre, the Sixteenth of September, just like the Fifth of May, so the mariachis were playing loud when you were born. The nuns lived there for a while after it stopped being a hospital, but now it's a Burger King.

Nogales. The town was something in those days, and exciting to me. Sometimes I'd go out walking, and I pushed you everywhere. We had no car. I used to walk all over with you, including buying all our vegetables across the line at the mercado. We'd buy papayas and vegetables and fruits—grapes. Sometimes your father would come, and he used to go to the Three Pigs barbershop to get haircuts. Your Aunt Norma took you there for your first haircut, and we saved one of your curls. We spent a lot of time across the line doing things.

On this side, I would take you to the park, which had a pond full of goldfish. I took you there almost every afternoon, until Tommy was born. Wherever I went you went. Whenever your father was home, he went, I went, and you went. We were always together.

Except when we went to the movies. We didn't have enough money for a babysitter, so we'd take turns going to the movies. They made a lot of movies around Nogales, and we used to see the stars sometimes. I saw John Wayne many years later when I was working at the hospital. I'll never forget one time when Tommy was in my arms. We walked into the Nogales Theater to watch Joseph Cotton in "The Bottom of the Bottle" and it started with someone walking into the Nogales Theater. It was funny. We watched them make the movie, and then went to see it.

We went to the Nogales Theater mostly, on Morley, but there was the Roxy and the Star too, on Grand Avenue. And across the line there was the Obregón and others. In England we used to go to the show at 3:00 in the afternoon, but the air was black because there was so much fog. We had to inch our way and hold hands to go.

❀

That year you were born things were happening. There was the big election for president. The town's newspaper, the Inter-national, *had a blackboard outside their office where they'd write all the election results. Everyone would gather when Mr. Pottinger would write the tallies. He did that for years, and that's where people would go to get the news.*

That was in November. At the beginning of 1953, after you were born, Mr. Dexter sold us a little, green, two-door car, but I don't remember what it was called. We started taking you to the drive-in movie, the El Rancho. It was one dollar for a car. One night they had an all-spooky night, and we stayed to about three in the morning watching movies.

That year your father went to work for the government, working on the United States–Mexico Boundary Commission. The president, though, Eisenhower now, was starting to cut down on this kind of work, and your father started looking.

Did I ever tell you this? You never used to call me mother or mom or mama. You would go down to Mrs. Barker's house, near the end of Rodriguez Street. She had six kids, who were always saying mamá this and mamá that to her, and that's what you would say. Then they would come to our place and they would say Agnes this and Agnes that, and that's what you would call me, too.

And you would go to their house in one outfit and come back in another. Mrs. Barker was always making you outfits—she dressed you as a charro, and in guayaberas. And sometimes she dressed you as a girl.

You would run through the neighborhood in diapers. "Where are you going?" I would ask.

"I'm going to Mama Barker's, Agnes," you would say.

Mrs. Barker made great beans, with so much cheese when you lifted it up it looked like pizza. I hadn't had pizza yet, but that's what I would think when I ate it—this pizza looks like Mrs. Barker's beans.

You ate beans, and so did Tommy. It started with the juice from beans, which was full of iron. We'd put some in your bottles. Your father would give you a chicken bone to suck, too, and it made you happy. You ate different kinds of cereal, Cream of Wheat, oats. Lots of Cream of Wheat. This would come back when your father got sick.

He would peel grapes for you, and pop them in your mouth.

Can you imagine that? He peeled your grapes. You were like that sometimes. Like, you couldn't have your formula milk sweetened with Karo syrup like everybody else—you were allergic. So we used to have to buy a special powdered stuff that cost almost a dollar a day which was a fortune. Tommy, on the other hand, he was breast-fed till he was at least two. He'd go out and play, come in for a meal, and run back out.

❀

The year Tommy was born, 1955, "Oklahoma" was made near Nogales. I remember one day I was pushing you both in a stroller and Gordon McRae walked right by the side of me and then in front of me. He was the one who sang "Oklahoma." They made the corn part in Elgin and around there, because I guess the corn that year in Oklahoma wasn't big enough to look as high as an elephant's eye. It was as low as an elephant's toe.

The next year, 1956, they were looking for someone to take over the Coca-Cola distributing job. Your father got it. Around that time I used to push you over to the Coca-Cola warehouse, which wasn't far from the house. They moved it later to the one you remember on Wayside Drive. I used to unload the Coca-Cola truck while he loaded it, and you used to sort the bottles—the Sunrises, the Nehis, the Cokes. And there were strawberry sodas, and some others. It's why we named our dog Cokey.

We used to take you every Sunday to Sonoita during the horse races and rodeos. I sold Cokes to Governor Pyle. Your father did such a good business that no other sodas came into town, and he ended up working for Coke about four years.

Then he figured—well, he knew—he couldn't get any further, no matter how good he did. It was, you know, because your father was Mexican.

We had fun those years, though. We would take you guys across the line on Sunday afternoons and we'd park outside the Recreo Bar. Your father would have a beer, a Superior or a Tecate, and they would bring out botana for us, which was like snacks, only really good—birria in fresh tortillas. I would hold your brother in my arms and try not to let any juice fall on him.

Well, we got married in 1951 and lived five years in the apartment. Near the end of that time, we would walk down to Mr. Larriva's store, which was the first store to get television in town. He had a tv in the window and everyone would stop and watch, forgetting what they were doing. They'd stay for a half-hour at least, eight or nine people across and five deep.

❀

We moved into the new house then, in Valle Verde, about four miles north of town and next to a big cow field. One of the first things I started doing was making tamales with Mary from next door. It took two days.

I know what you remember, too. We used to make some tamales with no meat at all, just masa, for all you kids. You didn't always like the things in the regular tamales. And we made bean tamales, too, which were sweet.

We had to be careful, though, of what you ate. One night when Tommy was about two he had been playing with a pretty big balloon. I went in the bedroom to check on you guys and I saw that Tommy's cheeks were bulging. I started to pull this black thing out and it was the balloon. I got the whole balloon out of his mouth. He could have choked to death. Well, but he didn't, and he did about a hundred things like that.

I remember I was cleaning house one day when you came in and told me that Tom had eaten all the berries off the pyracantha bush. I didn't know whether they were poisonous or not, so I gave Tommy saltwater to drink, and he threw up all over the place. Of course I found out later that they weren't poisonous. Poor guy. It was like that sometimes. We all had to learn together.

About 1962, your father got a job at the courthouse doing everything—the court librarian, bailiff, probation officer, and everything else. That's how the job was. He later became the chief probation officer, and sat exams for certification as a legal translator, and for a while was one of only four certified in the state. He translated for the Mexican Supreme Court. He worked for twenty years there.

During all this time when you were boys I didn't work yet myself. I was taking care of the house and you. But I'll tell you, I started missing some things.

I couldn't get the English pastries. There were so many, and nothing like them here. Pastries are what I missed, and English chocolate. Black Magic Chocolates. They were so good. You would get a regular selection of chocolates—all kinds. The mixture was common, but the taste was so different. Black Magic and Cadbury's. Cadbury's would make Aero chocolate bars, and they would melt away in your mouth. Some were a penny, and some were twopence—two pennies, depending on the size.

You always got selection boxes at Christmas. You always got one, but the size depended on how rich your parents were. We would always get a two and six pence box. You got the selection box with your gift, but sometimes it was better.

And I really missed the little white sugar pigs with pink around their ears and snouts, and a little string for a tail. We paid a halfpenny for them. And marzipan in all shapes, but mostly marzipan flowers.

❀

We ended up buying our tv from Mr. Kaanta. He came and installed it, with a huge antenna. He said the house would blow down before the antenna would go, and he was right. When cable came a few years ago, we took the antenna down ourselves, and it was still perfectly good. The whole neighborhood used to look like a bay full of sailboats, with all those antennas.

But we got a tv. It was a big tin tv. We were the first ones in the neighborhood, and all the kids used to come in and watch Laurel and Hardy. I went to the "Wizard of Oz" when it first came out at the movies, and so I made you watch it when it came on television. We watched that movie every year they showed it. And they had a scary movie every Saturday night, which everybody in the world still remembers.

In 1961, for our tenth wedding anniversary, Tommy split his face open by running into one of the neighborhood kids. We had to take him to the Nogales Clinic and get him fixed up. Remember we have that picture of him with that big black eye? He didn't cut his cheek, he split it.

I wasn't unused to this, of course, but it's different when it's your own child. I had trained as a nurse at the Royal Warrington Infirmary. When I came here there was too much to do at home. I had you and Tommy, and between the two of you I had a tubal pregnancy and a miscarriage. I did home nursing for a while, taking care of one of the doctor's mothers.

In about 1963 I started working for one of the surgeons, Dr. Noon, on the back street just off Grand, right next to the border. I worked for Dr. Noon off and on for about three years. Then I went to work at the hospital for three years, and then I went to work for Dr. Moody at the Nogales Clinic, for thirteen years. I was off for a few months, but then I helped Dr. Suarez open his office. I worked for him about ten years. I retired to enjoy myself, but four months after I did your father got sick. You know the rest.

During those years when I was working, I couldn't always cook like I did, and you had to fend for yourselves a lot. I know we had so many tv dinners, and when we got that Veg-o-matic all you wanted was French fries. And hamburgers, no matter what. Even when we traveled all over Mexico, all you wanted was hamburgers.

But Sunday mornings were always a bigger breakfast—crêpes suzette. I would mix flour, egg, and milk into a thin paste, which I'd then pour, a little at a time, into the pan to make crêpes. Then I'd squeeze fresh lemon juice on and sprinkle sugar over them as well and roll them up. You and Tommy would eat a dozen each of those things, and then lie around all morning moaning.

And sometimes I'd still make cream puffs. They were mostly flour and eggs, eggs whipped until they turned shiny, and a little water. I'd slit them when they were done and fill them with whipped cream.

Do you remember when your father used to carry a gun? It's funny how I just thought of that. For a long time in the Sixties, while he was working at the court—he had become the chief probation officer by now, among all those other things—your father became a United States Commissioner. That was like a Justice of the Peace, only for federal things. We didn't know if he'd get the job because he was Mexican, but he did. He might have been the only one. But it was the Sixties, and all the drug stuff was starting, and it was all federal. He was the judge for all that stuff at the border, and in all his years of doing it they only overturned two of his decisions.

Well, they made him a deputy sheriff, too, and that's why he carried a gun. Only he didn't wear it every day. Just when things got dangerous. Do you remember the time they tried to kill your father? We were eating across the line at The Cavern, and when he went to the bathroom some guys got him and started to take him outside with their guns in his back. It was lucky there were some off-duty police who knew us and who were eating there, too. I got them right away when I saw those guys taking your father outside, and the police went running after them. They threw your father down and started shooting at each other. You were both home asleep, and didn't even know.

When the judge was retiring in the early Eighties, your father decided to run for Justice of the Peace. That worked out so well, and it's what he did for the next eleven years, until he got sick.

For the longest time, Nogales just reached to Villa Coronado, where your elementary school was. The disposal plant was only a little ways down. You could walk across the line anytime. But I guess we were part of the change when we moved. There used to be an ice plant, but it's closed now. It was at the side of where Dr. Suarez's office was. It was right in there, and part of it used to cross over the street to the railroad, and water used to drip down onto the cars from the melting ice. And there was a dry cleaners, on Grand Avenue, but it burned down. It had a lot of pipes coming out of the top, for the steam to come out. And your father's family used to live on Torres Street, at the top. You can see it in the old maps, but they tore it down for the freeway.

❀

Your father asked for this a week or so before he died. Please would I make it, he said. This was illegal in terms of his diet, but it didn't much matter. Even the doctor told me that, now. He was eating lots of Cream of Wheat, like in the early days, and it made him feel good. But this time, he wanted something that was something.

Chilaquiles. I made them like I always did, even though we hadn't had any in a long time. First in one pan I got the tortillas in little pieces and fried them just a little, just lightly. In another pan I had already fried garlic, red chile, chicken stock, and a lot of yellow cheese, though sometimes I used to use white. The last time before this was white cheese. That all got poured on top of the tortillas and then I let them cook awhile. He liked it so much.

Well, I'm enjoying some things now, myself. I found some gooseberry jam.

I never told you this, but did you know I was told by some friends in England that if I came over here I would have to walk on one side of the street with your father and the white people would walk on the other side? It's true. I was also told that if we got a house all of your father's family would move in with us because they were Mexican.

Your father said that he got into a lot of places because of me. He didn't think he would have gotten into them because of who he was and how he looked. Restaurants, stores, just places. It happened to him a lot, and I know because I saw it. Places that gave free samples, you know, they would completely ignore your father, and so we never went back to them.

But mostly I don't feel that people were prejudiced toward us. We got along with everybody and I tried to be nice to everybody and anything I could do for anybody I did. But you do realize, you know, your father and I never had any close friends, did we? No couples, nobody. We had each other. Ruth Beatty came over and played Monopoly.

But Mrs. Barker was like my second mother, more than your grandmother. Your grandmother and I were okay, but not really very close. It was hard, but okay. Mrs. Barker was the one who really helped me. And we never belonged to clubs. We felt that we didn't want to do what clubs made you do. We didn't want to be tied down to meetings or anything. Following rules had never helped us anyway.

When I was here I just decided if I was going to live here I was going to do as the Romans do and go day by day. That's just what I had to do. I realized I was not in England anymore where you had tea and crumpets every day at 4:00. I was going to live just the way they lived in Nogales. I decided this before I came over here. I decided this was another world I was coming to and I would have to make my life in this new world. I knew absolutely nothing about this country or the people or the food. All I knew was your father. I was kind of scared and kind of not, because I knew your father would be there all the time for me. It was enough.

RADIO KNOG

It was a Saturday night and I don't know where my father was and my brother must have already been asleep. But my mother was there. Me and my mother and the green Zenith Moderne, which was usually a kitchen radio, but tonight, tonight it was a living room radio. February 25, 1964. It was the Sixties already on the calendar, but it was still the Fifties here in Nogales.

Sonny Liston was fighting, and we were ready. Sonny Liston and Cassius Clay, some guy who talked a lot and made us laugh because we couldn't believe what he was saying, and how loud he was saying it. He was shouting that he was the greatest and had a pretty face and stuff that nobody said, not about themselves. It made us wrinkle our foreheads and shake our faces from side to side. It made us do what we imagined they would do to each other, only we were laughing.

It was me and my mother listening to the Sonny Liston–Cassius Clay fight, the heavyweight boxing championship of the world. My mother didn't like boxing, really, but she liked to yell when she could and when it was all right and didn't scare anybody. She went to wrestling matches and bullfights for the same reason. We shouted through the match, but there was more to the moment. This particular evening it wasn't boxing, so much as that this was just something big. It's the *big* we were listening to. It was the Fifties and it was a nice night and that's what we did on it.

Even though Mr. Clay, as my mother called him, made us laugh and wrinkle ourselves up, we still couldn't believe he won the fight, and that was the thing. You felt good and you felt bad, all at the same time, but not like two sharp pains—more like two bowls of water floating around inside you, two lakes. They were both water, but you knew they didn't mix. Something was right and something was wrong and that was boxing.

That, and my mother saying she might just run away with Mr. Clay some day if she felt like it. Just like that.

This was all somehow tied in to how, years later, she had a Saturday morning television ritual for me and my brother, all of us watching Tarzan movies, eating barbecue potato chips, and drinking tomato juice. It made us feel great because we never heard of anybody else doing that. This was ours.

The television, through no coincidence, was a Zenith, too. The world worked that way, my parents acting as if they had a personal relationship with this company, just like they had with Electrolux and Chevrolet. It's not like somebody from the company ever called them up or corresponded with them. It just felt like they thought somebody might, and my parents wanted to be able to say they got it right.

We turned the radio off after the match was done. That's what people did in those days, turn the radio off. You didn't keep it on and listen for an analysis or a post-show summary or anything like that: If it was finished, you turned it off. I've forgotten that, now that I watch pre-game reports on sports shows and political analyses of election results that go on all night.

Seven o'clock and you watched it and then you turned it off. The Fifties.

It's like that in movies and television programs, but it's plot there. The characters get some information from the newscaster and then they turn it off so they can speak. But we were the characters, then. We still are, I guess, so that it's only a matter of time before we start seeing television shows where the people turn on the news to get some information and then, instead of turning it off so they can speak, they leave it on, and we get swept into some endless video vortex, some film loop, which has us by the eyes and won't let us go.

I remember that radio of ours from when I was smaller, too. I remember it for its moments, little lines of something that mattered would just come out of it, little blooms from the green stem. I remember listening one morning to the Arthur Godfrey show when all of a sudden there was a bulletin and the announcer said that Amelia Earhart's crash sight had been found. It wasn't true exactly, but they said it anyway, and I remember.

It's also where my mother hid my brother's bottle one day when she said the time had come for him to give it up. She showed me as she hid the bottle behind the radio and then when my brother came into the kitchen she said she had given it away, that another little boy had come by and needed it so she gave it to him, and my brother said all right, and that was it. He never asked about a bottle again.

Our town's radio station was KNOG, for K-Nogales, I think. It was one of those stations where, if you called with the right answer, you got a free record. My mother was good at it, at right answers to those radio questions, as if they were aimed right at her, like What goes into plum pudding? Or, What is a beefeater? It was almost as if the deejays were talking just to her. But what they were doing was asking questions about the most foreign place they could think of in this small Arizona town on the border of Mexico—England.

We eventually had a pile of 78s that was enviable.

On the other hand, it probably wasn't a coincidence that the station was moving in the main toward 33⅓s. Seventy-eights weigh a ton, if you've ever held one. Having my mother come down once a week for her ten or twenty records probably saved them a fortune in movers' costs.

But our radio was a good radio, and always right in the middle of important things in those days. The world worked with the radio part of it: Something happening? Quick—turn on the radio. They were that much a part of us, but I don't see radios anymore. They're always part of something else, and their sound doesn't sound like a radio at all.

These radios, this thing of turning them on, for big things and for small things too, and for music: It was an absolute but transitory mathematics. Turn on the radio and something will happen. It was an equation, but just for a while, just for a half-century.

My grandparents on my father's side,
Refugio and Margarito, with two
young cousins. My grandfather always
appeared stern, and the look rubbed off on
those around him. But don't believe it—
there was a life inside that look.

PART 5

PIG COOKIES EVERYWHERE

I never liked pig cookies very much. In fact, I hated them. But they were what you got growing up along the border—pig cookies at birthday parties, on Christmas, Saints' days, and the rest. Pig cookies were part of our child's litany of sweets, along with the light brown, near-liquid bars of fudge, the *cajeta*, and *ciruelas*, and those little plastic packets of colored, sugar-and-chili *tamarindo*. But because the gingerbread cookies looked like pigs, well, that was the thing. Who could resist them, lying fresh-made on a tray in the bakery.

And that's all it took: As a child, if you laughed, just once, at someone dangling a pig cookie in front of you, then the whole family from then on thought they were your favorite. Because of that, they've been around for centuries. Ask anyone.

Cochitos, they are called in Mexico, and people still say— "remember how you used to like *cochitos?*"

But I never did. I liked the chewy *cajeta* much better, even if I didn't know what it was, exactly. I even liked the vague taste of the balsa-wood box the *cajeta* came in, whose top you would have to break in half and then use as a spoon to get the stuff out.

But gingerbread is gingerbread. You might like other things better, all right. You might like them a lot better. But pig cookies—you don't forget pig cookies.

❀

My grandmother used to tell me that the day my father was born the volcano Tacaná erupted a few miles down from the house in which they were living. She told the story different ways, but some things stayed the same. They were in the town of Tapachula in Chiapas, at the southernmost tip of Mexico and right near the border with Guatemala. She remembers that the house had large windows, which they needed for breezes in the heat of the tropics. Their sills were large, like benches, and she used to sit on them sometimes, as if they were just more chairs in the house. And of course the sills had doilies. She didn't say that, but I knew.

My grandmother told me many times that what she remembered most from that day was the hundreds of birds in all colors and sizes that flew into the house through those windows, tearing right through the mosquito nettings, and perching themselves up on the sapling rafters, and how the noise they made became for her the loud noise my father made as he was being born, and her own crying as well. It was a noise that was loud, and long, a whole afternoon. The story was old, but I would think of these birds many years later when I went to eat Chinese food. The restaurant there had a birdcage from the floor to the ceiling, inside. The noise of the birds became part of what we ate.

My father's family was living in Tapachula at that time because my grandfather, Margarito, was inextricably involved in the Mexican Revolution, and he kept his family at the far edges of the Republic—in the northern Nogales and the southern Tapachula—so that, in case his side lost, the family might take just one more step and be quickly in another world.

The boat in which my father's family had sailed to Tapachula from a point higher up on the coast sank the day they got there. My grandmother tells me how, floating in the bay, she was rescued, and how as she floated all she could hear were the three band members on the boat playing the only thing they could think of, "*Mas cerca mi dios a ti*," and then how she could not hear them, only people crying and chickens.

The boat they came on had sunk. The boat they would take to leave would not come. But it was not just my grandmother there waiting for her husband to come home happy or dead. The side stories of revolution were there in Tapachula, a whole town of displaced people put on hold, taken out of time, not so different from the Nogales in which I was raised, and where the rest of the family was waiting. Nogales was on the opposite side of Mexico, on the border with Arizona. Nogales and Tapachula were, for my family, both the same town. They were towns next to countries, but inside countries as well.

❀

The day my father was born, the president of Mexico at the moment, Alvaro Obregón, on whose side my grandfather Margarito had been fighting, was to come to Tapachula and christen my father, who had been named in his honor, Alvaro Alberto. He would have come because Don Margarito was his right hand, in place of the one Obregón had literally lost in an earlier campaign. He would have come, but was assassinated. The future for my father, for his family, for that town, at that moment was unimaginable. 1928–29. The Thirties.

Tacaná had erupted in the state of Chiapas, near Tapachula. The stock market in the north would crash. Hitler's war would come to Mexico in boats. Augusto César Sandino had taken hold to the south, his Sandinistas fighting U.S. Marines. He would be assassinated by the first Somoza. Leon Trotsky, banished from Russia, would come here to be assassinated, and the schoolchildren—my father—would learn the "Internationale" so that he might be remembered. Pancho Villa, Alvaro Obregón, Venustiano Carranza, each a side of the revolution, had all been assassinated. Artaud would come here and catch the theater of cruelty in his head, and Breton, and all the others, everyone from the edge.

It was a mutual attraction. Everything was nothing. There was nowhere else to go, but one could not stay here.

❀

This is all mine, what I inherit, even the name, but backward, Alberto Alvaro, because everything was turned around, and the name had to come out that way. I was born of people who were outside time and place, people who were displaced and unsure, people reduced ultimately to manners rather than to laws for survival. They found the line inside themselves, the things they would and would not do, in there. Their lives are from before the border fences.

This was my family—Margarito, Refugio, Clemente, Ventura, and all of them—a people between wars, between cultures, between governments. They didn't need a fence to tell them this. The churches in Mexico had been closed down but did not disappear. The Chinese had been deported, but had not gone. The Depression and the stock market crash had happened in the United States, but now the United States was everywhere, and what happened there happened to everyone. The border finally was not a fence. It was the decade of the Thirties itself.

If there was uncertainty in those years, there was also its opposite. It was the law of physics. The everyday was still the everyday: A toothache was still a toothache, and a pig cookie, well. These were the constants from the realm of certainty. The seasons, the circus, a good dinner at the finish of a day.

This was the gingerbread of living. In the years when the circus came, everything seemed possible, as anyone could see that walking the high wire had little to do with the confines of a canvas tent. If the people were uncertain, the performers were bold. If there was, in sum, general disaffection in this world and in this place, there could also be found a wild love for two clowns, for an elephant and a couple of horses.

LA CALERA

I know only this little bit about our family ranch in Mexico, which was called *La Calera*, which means "lime seller," or "lime maker"—it refers to the mineral lime that comes from the ground, though all my life, when people said "lime," I associated it with the fruit. It is a name which keeps its own secrets, and whose explanation I cannot further. "*La Calera*," my family would say about the *ranchito*, but they would never say more or why: "That's just its name, *La Calera*," they would say, as if it were enough. It was that way with a lot of things.

But they did tell the story of my grandmother's uncle Carlos, who was a stern man, perhaps even cruel had he not been a member of the family and so could not be referred to as such. It was on this ranch that he taught my grandmother and her sisters to swim. He tricked them this way and that, until he got them to a small stream, where he made them all get in the water and start to swim. Every day for a whole summer he hit them with a small branch from a mulberry tree until they swam, even though they would come home with bruises and welts. They became good swimmers.

Then one day Uncle Carlos decided that my grandmother should not only ride a horse, but ride one very well. This is how he was about things. He enticed my grandmother, who in those days as a teenager had long hair and thick, all the way down her back, onto a large horse, and then he handed the baby Pirrín, my uncle, up into her arms. Everyone agreed, on that day and all the way to now, that Pirrín was a beautiful baby. My grandmother held him with attention, and so could not hold the reins of the horse.

Uncle Carlos, with the same switch he had used to teach my grandmother and her sisters to swim, hit the haunches of the horse, and it went off at a gallop. My grandmother kept herself and the baby upright, and could not have done otherwise, so much was her upbringing. Uncle Carlos laughed, and the others watching screamed, but my grandmother made no sound, save perhaps for a low purr exchanged with the boy charged to her arms.

At a distance but still within view of the ranch house, the horse—whose own name, unlike *La Calera*, is lost to the years—because it was unguided, ran underneath a tree with low branches as some horses will to get the flies and beetles off their backs. The tree swept up my grandmother by her hair into its own arms.

The horse kept running and went on to stumble and kill itself, but my grandmother stayed, hanging there, with the baby folded to her. She hung by her long, thick hair, which had tangled and wisped into the tree. She hung there and did not move, and the baby did not cry.

When the others came to her rescue, they had to cut her hair to get her out of the tree. She never grew it long again, and Uncle Carlos, who kept his hair very short, went on to live by himself as the keeper of an orchard near Magdalena in Sonora.

I visited that orchard once, as a child. We stopped there in the springtime, and all the fruit in all the trees hung there spectacularly, and every tree was as good as a painting. But I also remember there was a sadness in Uncle Carlos's eyes, something, though the taste of the peaches and apricots, of the nectarines and the lemons, the taste was everything good. It was those limes I always thought of when I heard the name of the ranch, *La Calera*. It was the limes in the trees, not the lime in the earth, that stayed with me, though it was a confusion of words.

I have one picture of him, Uncle Carlos black and white and looking straight ahead, the top button buttoned on his old white shirt and his head cocked a little to the side. That's it. But I have many pictures of my grandmother, all of them with short hair and a seriousness, whether she liked it or not, equal to her uncle's.

MY FATHER AND THE SNOW

My father is dying. There it is, openly said.

It is a long and slow worm, this thing of dying in the way that he is. But it is his dying, his alone and no one else's. And that is the particular—toward which end can be fairly said that he has been an ordinary man who has colored outside the lines of all of his lives, and of the lives around him, and in doing so has written with his life for himself a striking story, worthy in its words and too fleet on its pages.

But what a serious-sounding debris of words. It's just that there's nothing else to say or to use. When I talk to my father these days, I think I am not very good with words. The reason is simple—when we used to talk together, we never talked very much about him, not the inside him. We looked at his architecture, but not who lived in it.

The outside him, the structure, the public him, that's what he gave me, and that's what much of my own literary work has been about. He was born near the end of the 1920s in southern Mexico, on the border of Guatemala, where there's a great deal of trouble right now, and where perhaps there has always been trouble. My grandmother's old but good story of him being born is equal to that drama—the volcano Tacaná erupting on his birthday, the birds from the surrounding jungle flying in through the open windows of their house, the noise they made being like the noise my father made as he was being born, and so on. The stories about my father, and about his father before him, are like that, full of old-style drama and told over and over again.

But the quieter sense of himself, that is something else. I don't finally understand very much about it. Nothing I can say about him, about his inside, comes easily or with authority. But I know the signs, the dodges he has used through the years, the small glimpses and half-looks, perhaps because I have inherited them in one form or another for myself. If I have seen him look to the side for a moment, in a particular circumstance, I have been able, sometimes, to know why, though not from anything he has ever told me.

❀

I take as measure against these recent days the fine drama and big lives of my parents together—that's where my father is still big. He, as I say, was born in Mexico, and my mother was born in England. How they met is another story altogether. What matters is that she came by herself across the ocean halfway around the world to be his wife, even though in her life up to then she had never been more than two train stops away from home.

Guglielmo Marconi, the inventor of the wireless telegraph, sent the single letter "S" through the air across the Atlantic in the 1800s. It was a first ephemeral traveler through an air of mystery. When I first read this, I thought of my mother, how she was this one letter coming from one place to another and hoping she would find a like alphabet, a place for herself, someone to reach up and catch her out of the air. Both the sending of the letter and my mother's coming over to this country were fleeting, even capricious acts, but they changed forever the worlds they would find.

That she would come, that he could catch her in flight, that he could hold on: These are as well something of the measure of my father, how by understanding something of my mother I understand something more of him. I don't for a moment diminish my mother in all of this. What is simply remarkable for me is this way of understanding—of understanding her, of course, but of understanding him too. He simply did these things, and it is a real measure.

The escape velocity of an object from earth is 7 mi/sec. If my father is revving up for his own act of travel, and I believe he is, it's hard to see because he seems to be moving so slowly. But the movement I think is all within, which says something about the inside of this man. That inside is a strong place. That is not something he ever needed to tell me.

Watching my father now I am too much reminded of this place my parents, my brother, and I have lived these many years, of its quieter and more secret underside, an underside one would only know by living here and paying attention. In this place that we live—my West, my father's North, and my mother's new hemisphere—rabbits in a burning field of grass can catch on fire. They run to a clear place where there is no fire, but, in doing so, light it up because their fur is burning. That way, in trying to save themselves, they spread the fire more. Dying like that is a difficult thing to watch. In slow motion, it is cruelty. And it spreads to everyone.

❁

I got news last night that my father was not doing well. My mother called, and she sounded clear—a rarity, as my parents like to put on the speaker-phone and have everybody talk. It never works out quite right, though, and my mother has a hearing aid anyway. So everybody shouts, and nobody hears, and sentences always go about half their intended distance. But that's family.

My mother wasn't on the speaker-phone, though, and she said my father was sleeping. Of course he wasn't. He was listening anyway from the couch—I could see it, like I'd seen it a hundred times in that house. He has diabetes, fully engaged, and had a stroke a little while back, which required that he have eye surgery. But this wasn't that.

He had been short of breath for a couple of days, so my mother—who was a nurse and still is, most days, except when my father can talk her into giving him just a little something, a little something he shouldn't be eating, which really he can do any time he likes, that's the truth of it, the good truth, my mother saying a little piece like that, she's sure it won't hurt his diet—my mother took him to the doctor, her former employer, who right away put her to work.

The nurse there had taken my father's blood pressure, but the doctor wanted my mother to take it. What he really wanted was for her to *feel* it, something he knew she'd understand, so that he wouldn't have to tell her something like 220 over 120, which was so much nothing. She felt it all right. And that meant my father felt it, too, them having been married so long.

The doctor ordered blood work, an EKG, and some small stuff, and then sent them to the hospital for a chest X-ray, just to be on the safe side. They went and got it done. Just to be on the safe side.

The results were in by afternoon. The EKG showed what it had shown before, the stroke, the little strokes before that. The X-ray was okay, showing the scarring around the heart from the stroke. But the blood work. "That was the thing," said my mother.

"His kidneys are only working at 20 percent," she said, quiet and matter-of-fact.

I listened to her, to how quiet she was. I don't know what you do with information like that. I have worked in a hospital. I know things. But none of that helped now.

"So, what do you think?" I asked.

"Well, the doctor has put him off salt, and off potassium. No more banana bread for a while. No more chile either."

"No more chile?"

"No, can you believe that?"

I knew my father was listening, the way she said this one.

"Then they're going to do it all over again on Friday. We'll know more then. I just wanted to call you because I thought you should know."

"Yes, that's right. I'm glad you called."

"I don't think I'm going to call your brother yet, do you think? I don't want to get him worried."

"No, no, you don't need to do that. We should see what happens on Friday." She knew I would call him.

Then my mother moved a little on the couch. I could hear it.

"Oh, your father's awake. Do you want to talk to him?"

"Sure."

"I'll just put this thing on so he can hear you. There. Can you hear?"

"Hi, son."

"Hi." I realize, every time, that I still don't know what to call him. "How are you feeling?"

"A little under the weather."

"I guess so. No salt, huh?"

"No salt. You should be careful."

"I will. Maybe I should think about no salt too. Well, I'll call on Friday."

❀

The process of diabetes is different for everyone, but ultimately and inexorably fierce, as it has been for my father. He has had a stroke, and kidney failure, dialysis, congestive heart failure, and all the rest, underscored by an itching all over that cannot be scratched enough. My father has finally lost his sight, and much else.

But it has been the loss of his sight that he cannot reconcile. He describes it as having woken up one day and suddenly not being able to get his bearings. And no matter how hard he rubs his eyes, fully expecting that the film will lift, they do not come back. He has kept trying for months, maybe now a year. He knows the center, from so many years of having been there, but he can't get back to it.

The way these things go is predictable enough, and any single day becomes the gauge.

The next time something happens, it's like the last time, only more. He has a blood infection, they said months later, but it's under control. The only thing we have to hope now is that he doesn't get another fever.

But of course, once said, that was the next thing.

And the next.

He has a heart problem, said the cardiologist. Cardiologist. I didn't even know he had a cardiologist.

It's an act of translation, the cardiologist said, like this: If you can understand what the diabetes has done to his eyes, that's what it's doing to his heart.

The diabetes has made him blind. I see that. What happens to the heart is more difficult to articulate, but not hard to understand. I see that, too.

❀

This last trip my father did what he's been doing for most of our last trips—he slept. He sleeps more than possible, maybe less than necessary. We talk around him in his chair, and do things that need doing, but it's all small. My aunt calls, long distance, and my father says a few words, but that's it. All of this is how things are now. That, and with us thinking a little too far ahead.

My mother is getting the house fixed up. She has had several slabs of concrete poured, an addition to the garage put up, a small fence added to the front yard. She can't stop fixing the house. And this thing of fixing the house—it works. It works and it's something she can do. She can't fix my father.

My mother has also been putting whipped cream on her doughnuts. And for dinner the cafeteria people at the hospital made her a fresh big batch of French fries, and she had only a little piece of pumpkin pie for dessert. She tells me this and things like this in bits and pieces of conversation, when she can't quite hold all the food in and it comes out as conversation.

My mother was a nurse, and that turns out to be a good thing for my father. But for all those years of working, she could always go home at the end of a day. She can't go home now, not like that. Hers has become a curious retirement, as if she never left work at all, and can't. It's like a dream, that way. And with arthritis as the electricity that powers it.

She would never call this whole thing with my father a *bad* dream. It's not in her. But she's been hard at work filling in those places in her that might have started to think it.

❀

My father always told me a story about snow, and how he en-
countered it for the first time when he visited Nogales, Arizona, from all the way down in the tropics, where snow was not
even a word. When in Nogales and as snow began to waft its
way down as it did so often in December in those days, in the
1930s, my father thought at the time that the sky was falling.
Given his record on these sorts of disasters, he worried that
perhaps he was responsible in some way. It would not be the
first time.

But his mother laughed, and told him it was snow. She said
it quickly and just like that, one word. Normal and regular.
She didn't even breathe fast. This made snow normal and regular, he supposed, which was factually true. But snow, however,
in Spanish, is the word *nieve*, which is also the word for ice
cream—and the only word he had for what he was seeing.

The stories he told when he got back to the tropics became
legend, especially as he had brought back a postcard with a
house surrounded by snow. In the United States, *nieve* comes
down from the sky, really. That's when he would show the
postcard. It comes down in *vainilla* up there, he would say. And
in later years, sometimes in *chocolate* as well.

This last time I saw my father in the hospital, he looked
snowed upon. These days his hair seems even whiter, his skin a
little darker, so that this time his hair seemed to be placed there,
almost to have fallen onto this place, rather than to have grown
out of it. That was the first thing I noticed. But the second
thing was his eyebrows. His eyebrows, too, had turned a white
I had not seen before. They were big enough before this, but
now, with their white kind of neon, they looked tremendous.
This was the snow even more, and he looked like he had just
stepped in from the outside, like his brow held the snow the
way an overhanging roof does.

This moment, all this snow, it was England again, from all
the stories my parents had told me together. It was from another place in that moment.

I was reminded of an event several years ago. I was a visiting writer at Vassar College, and the college was gracious enough to fly my family out to be with me for my last week there. My son was instantly on fire in all of the wonder of the cold. Having grown up all of his six years in Arizona, he was an energy matching up to the newness of this landscape.

He was quiet enough about it. This was his secret. But he had found something, and it was big.

On the night before we were to leave, it was snowing. We put him to bed, and said our things. A little later that evening, I heard quiet but insistent sobs coming from his room. I went in and found him in tears. He said he didn't want to leave, and I understood him profoundly at that moment.

We talked awhile, and said some more things, and did what could be done. But I knew what had happened, I knew what the crying was about, and I have been haunted by it ever since. He had no name for what he felt. Instead, because he could not yet articulate his feelings, he let his body do his talking, and what it said, it said elegantly, and spoke beyond itself, as any honest word invariably must.

He met snow, and when he knew he had to leave it, he cried for beauty.

❊

In that moment, I did not want to be my son's father. I did not want to be the one who took him away from something he had found. It's a hard thing to explain.

Like that, my father too has been hard to explain. I can't say that my father was a father the way fathers are fathers, the way they are in books, in movies, even in songs—that's way too much father. And he wasn't like my grandfather, who was the center of life, overbearing, and just generally the head of all things on earth—my father didn't want to be that. My father had run away from home, after all. At fourteen, he had run away from his own larger-than-life father, from *papá*, from *papi*, from San Luís Potosí where they were living to Nogales on the border of a new country and a new world in a new time, from the good and the bad and the middle of it all. So, when the time came for my father to be the father, it had to be something different.

But that's the rub. My father became something inside the word, and around and between the word. He found a place in it that worked for him. But it wasn't *father*, exactly.

All of which is all right with me, except that now I don't know what to call him, and I haven't for a long time. Probably because of the English of my mother, or because it was the Fifties and it's what people said on television, and to be sure that it was not his old *papá* in a new world, I grew up calling my father *daddy*, and my brother still can say it with ease. But somewhere along the way, that became a hard word for me to say. The thing is, I could never replace it with anything equal. When I had to write something, or found some other circumstance that compelled me to call him something, I mumbled or said *dad* or took a left turn. I still do it, every telephone call and every visit.

Maybe after everything, this is my own discovery. This is my snow. I don't know what to call my father. Somewhere in my life he was *daddy* with authority and arms and life. It was simple and easy and it worked. I need an honest word like that to call him. I need back the ease of saying it right out of my mouth without a second thought.

THE PÉSAME

Along the border, when a person dies there are many rituals. The one I think of most is not itself so much a ritual as a name in Spanish for something people say to each other about how sorry they are that someone has died. They say this not just with a word, but with everything they have. At a wake, one takes the opportunity to go over to the widow and give her the *pésame*, as if it were a thing—*el pésame*, "the" *pésame*. Through the years I have given it to people, and they have given it back to me.

The *pésame* means something fairly straightforward, and so it is all the more devastating. The word is derived from *peso*, for weight, and *me*, for me, and the dictionary says it means "my deepest sympathy." But that's not what the word means.

It's more like *I feel the crush too*, or *it weighs on me as well*. This is what I remember most from funerals—going over to the widow—who herself becomes an object in this moment, "the" widow—going over to the widow and giving her the *pésame*, which is just the name for whatever you say in that moment, those few words—I'm sorry, or *así es la vida*, or, he was a good man. It's a few words, but a nodding of the head and the holding of a hand, maybe with a shrugging of the shoulders as well. That is the part not to forget, the nodding of the head or the shrugging of the shoulders. That's the part you have to have seen, and which no one can tell you.

This is a ritual seen all over Mexico and Latin America, but on the border the *pésame* is not just an understanding and recognition that death has come. It's also an understanding of life itself between two places. "I understand," someone might say. But on the border, this means: I understand where you came from, I know the *ranchito*, or I know the *pueblito*. I know what it took to get here, the immigration and so many tears so many times. I know that your husband has been taken away, but I know what you know: It's not just your husband, but his whole story that has been taken away.

This is what the *pésame* is on the border. Between life and death, between two countries, just always between. It's *this* life, of having come from so far and having worked so hard to get *here*. It's *this* life, and it is so much bigger than the body that lies in the coffin in front of us.

We both know this man used to ride a horse, and very well. But looking at him, who would think it now? Who will remember it? That is the *pésame*.

THE CARTOON MORTUARY

At my father's funeral, I met a friend whom I did not recall but whose family I knew well. He was older than I was, maybe ten years, and had left town well before I reached high school. We began to talk, because that is what happens. And we began to talk stories, which is the gift of a small town like Nogales, where people read newspapers differently.

That is, newspapers fool no one. The front of the paper is what's expected; the back of the paper is what's meaningful. It's on this page that the people of the town live and die, and get married, and have babies. This is almost always where we find ourselves most.

As we talked, he told me about his uncle who came to this country from Spain. The uncle fought somewhere over here in this hemisphere, but didn't go back, and went to Mexico instead, eventually traveling and ending up on Nelson Street in Nogales, which everybody knows was the street behind the big stores, or what used to be the big stores—LaVille's, Capin's, Bracker's, Kress.

The uncle opened up a cigar factory, though it was really just him and his brother, and the factory was not too much of a factory, really, though he liked the sound of the word and stuck by it. The enterprise worked for a while, but this uncle did not get along with his brother, who had also ended up on Nelson Street, curiously just around the time the first uncle was think-ing about opening the factory. The luck of this timing gave the undertaking an air of good sense.

But they fought constantly, and the proposition seemed doomed. The uncle, however, had an idea. He hired someone to read to the two of them as they worked. They both had to pay fair attention so as not to get lost in the story that was being read, and in this way they stopped fighting. Along the way they got some education out of this, too, which was a bonus.

As it turns out, I was telling this story in turn to another friend, who had just happened to be reading about the history of cigar making. Hiring readers, it seems, was a common practice. Whether this man in Nogales knew it or not, or invented it for himself, I don't know. I do know it was their own experience, finally, their own stories they heard, and heard together. That made it theirs.

As my friend and I were talking, I was remembering that side of town. Nelson Street was bounded on the one side by the border fence, and on the other by Carroon's Mortuary. It had its name made up in big silver letters above the door, and it looked like a movie studio, like MGM or Universal, the way you used to see production companies pictured in the old news-reels, with those letters above their gates.

When I was young, I didn't know what a mortuary was, but I did know what cartoons were, and that's the word I read as I looked up at that sign: Cartoon Mortuary. The movie theater was on Morley Avenue, the main street with the big stores, but I thought this was easily the better street because it was the place where they made the cartoons for the theater.

The mortuary seemed to me clearly the theater's warehouse, just like all the other big stores had warehouses behind them, plain enough. And I knew they kept all the stuff they used in the stores in the warehouses. You'd see all the stores' stuff as you drove along Nelson Street. So why not a cartoon factory, a cartoon warehouse, a place to store the cartoons for the Cinex movie theater in front? They had to make and keep the cartoons somewhere.

The owners of the mortuary finally moved it from Nelson Street to just outside the city limits, though they were soon annexed by the city—there was too much business not to tax them, I suppose. They moved the mortuary in the direction of where I lived, into an old house I had seen for many years. It was hidden a little among some limestone boulders, some mes-quite and brush, and some ancient oleanders. This spot was a fine place, for anything, even just for looking at.

When my father died last fall, Carroon's took care of the arrangements. It was the new mortuary, the house my father had passed at least as many times as I had.

That Carroon's took care of the arrangements went without saying. "Of course," you would say if you lived there. That's the way it is in a small town: no choices. No choices, like death, one might add. And though saying so and making that comparison might be tempting, it wouldn't be fair.

If there is an exasperation in having no choices, there is also an odd comfort in that knowledge, and a necessity to think that the mortuary people know what they're doing. After all, there is no alternative. It's a package deal.

To think otherwise would be too scary. To think that the mortuary, behind its walls, might have nothing more than the two men in the cigar factory, who might not get along all that well—this would be too much.

I don't think I would have handled choices very well at this point anyway. Helping my mother was enough. One mortuary, one death, one way to do it. Like that. It felt certain, and certain is strong, and strong is right. There was a small mathematics at work, a small-town physics.

In the midst of it all, however, I could not stop thinking about the Cartoon Mortuary, and wishing I had read its sign correctly, that it had indeed said "cartoon." The business of burying my father would have had a whole different feel. The humorous first impulse, of course, is how it makes me think of Porky Pig bursting out of the end credits of the cartoon and saying in his stutter, "That's all folks."

That's not really what I mean, the bad pun of those words, but I like the spirit of that connection between something so silly and something so somber. I like that cartoons helped me with that sense of connecting dots in the world, making connections one might not say aloud, but which catch the mind too hard at work in its seriousness.

Once upon a time cartoons took care of me. They made me laugh. They made me feel good. They showed up when I was five or six, and we got our first television, a big, tin, simulated blond-wood Zenith black and white, the kind with tubes.

Its color always made me wonder where there were blond trees. Maybe there was a whole blond-wood forest in Norway or somewhere that I didn't know about. I supposed because of this that there was still a great deal for me to learn in this world.

Still, at my father's funeral, there was no cartoon mortuary, no such place, except in me. Only I saw the cartoon, and thought, if only for a half-moment, to feel good.

I was the warehouse, finally. Not this place. And in that warehouse was something that remembered what I used to think, and how I used to see the world. At least for a while, cartoons became my readers, just like the readers the men in the cigar factory got. The cartoons gave me an education while I was getting an education. And for the while we watched them, my brother and I, and sometimes my parents, we all had something in common. It wasn't finally the cartoons. It was something instead that, in the midst of all our laughing, we invented for ourselves in those hours.

BREAKING PIÑATAS

The day came when my son, Joaquín, was old enough to recognize a birthday, and that he could get some pretty good stuff out of his parents, out of his friends, and out of strangers, even, if he were smart enough. And we got him everything it takes— the cake, the decorations, the invitations, the loot bags for his miniature thug gang of elves, who were all catching on to this party stuff pretty fast.

We got him all this—and, the piñata. A very large, turquoise and white and yellow Humpty Dumpty. Actually, my parents were the ones. They got him from across the line, Nogales, Mexico, and he was the real McCoy, this fine fellow, full of detail and energy. A Humpty among Humpties.

"I'm not going to hit it," he said.

We looked at him.

"You told me not to hit things."

We looked at each other. We had indeed said that to him, and more than once.

"But this is different, Joaquín," we said.

He burst into tears. "I'm not going to hit it," he said again.

There we all stood. The issue had come up before, and was always surprising. When he was a little younger, we had tried to keep toy guns away from him, until one day he approached us with the magnetic letter "L" in his hand, taken from the refrigerator. He held it just so, snuck up on us, and pointed.

"Bang," he said. "Bang bang."

"We better get him a gun," I said.

So here we were again, confronting the issue of violence, and what were we telling him? It's okay, son. Go right ahead and beat the living daylights out of Humpty, and here's a beautiful bat to do it with. Try it, it's fun.

It's possible that might be a little confusing.

We finally reached a compromise. We would keep Humpty safe and sound, and get him a Mickey Mouse that he and his friends could whack to pieces. Mickey, that was one thing. But Humpty, that was another. We couldn't explain it, and he couldn't explain it, but somehow it was okay.

He didn't seem to mind taking a few swings at Mickey, I think maybe because he thought Mickey could take it. He had seen enough cartoons to know this. That mouse could bend and jump, and even if he got it, got it BAD, he could *finger-snap* and put himself back together. Everybody knew that.

But in Humpty's story, things didn't turn out so well. If you hit Humpty and broke him, then that was that. Finding a single moral or message out of all this is not easy or clear. This comes out of childhood, after all. It's not clear, but it is strong, and our son was paying attention.

Don't hit, we told him, but showed him how to do it. Oh sure, we made him wear a blindfold, but then we cheered him on. I don't think I can figure it out any better than he could.

Once, at a piñata party in my neighborhood when I was a kid, a mother put a glass piggy bank into the piñata. I've never forgotten that. All the things that could have happened—glass splintering, all of us getting cut as we got down onto the ground with our hands and knees to grab the candy, the screaming, the blood swirling into the caramels.

I saw the thing come flying out when the piñata was finally broken. Nobody knew it was in there. It came flying out, and the moment was slow motion—the pig was moving in accident time. I watched it sail and arc and fall in a time so slow and rich that it still exists for me, right into a little boy's hands. Just like that. A glass piggy bank of terror, transformed into a moment incarnate, an unforgettable second, a smiling on that boy so big I thought the edges of his lips might move out past the sides of his face. It was a moment full of all the things that could have happened, and what did. Piñatas have been like that for me. I shouldn't have been so surprised by my son's reaction. Confusion—as he showed it to me—is the only thing that does make sense.

The boy got the pig, and it was a handsome pig, ready for pennies. That's just how it ended up, and everybody was happy.

SIR FRANCIS DRAKE AND ME

Very slowly, my father ran over me with a truck. I was three, and busy digging a fine hole in the hard dirt. The hole, it was a marvel: I had a spoon, and with it I had shaved off, and out, very carefully, layer after layer of the packed dirt, as if it were ice cream, frozen too hard.

I was in my own time at that moment and in my own world, so that my regular ears did not hear the regular world. They did not hear my father turning on the large, Coca-Cola delivery truck. He worked for Coca-Cola in those days, which had its benefits around dinnertime and if you were thirsty. This was before the world discovered sugar and calories.

The truck was fully loaded with hundreds of cases of soda, in hundreds of shades of color. It wasn't just the Coke, but grape Nehis and Sunset oranges as well, a litany of dark blues, oranges, browns, and the straw color of the cases with their red writing. My father looked behind the truck with his mirrors, and he looked in front of the truck but just straightforwardly. It was a snub-nose truck, and I was sitting right in front of its license plate, a spot he couldn't quite see or suppose that I would be in.

He thought my mother was taking care of me. My mother thought my father had me, that he was giving me a ride in the high cab as he often did.

The truck started, but I knew this sound and wasn't afraid. I looked at it, at the license plate, and I watched it begin to come forward. I felt it as the bumper gently pushed me at the chin, making me roll backward the way my parents had done with me hundreds of times on my bed.

I lay flat on my back and began to watch as the truck rolled over me. I saw its dark undersides, the wires and the oil, the turning gears. It was a show, and I was its audience.

Suddenly my mother screamed, and I started to lift my head up to see what had happened to her. I could see her face, looking at me underneath the truck. It looked awful, like something really bad had happened, but to her, so I started to cry.

There were no tragic consequences, and the story of my getting run over got told hundreds of times afterward, so much that I feel I remember it both as the child I was and the adult I am now. It is something that has stayed with me. My parents checked me over and checked me over, and checked again, but the answer was the same each time. I was all right. And I wouldn't even have been scared if my mother had not screamed like she did.

❀

Getting rolled over by a truck happens many different ways, and a truck has a bag full of disguises. You may not get hurt every time, though you cannot help but be changed.

Stationed in France just after the war, my father got Sundays off. Like so many other GIs, he was taken in by a French family for Sunday dinners, during which they were very generous. They invariably gave my father slices from the very center of the large loaves of the dinner's bread, which seemed to him an extraordinary gesture.

And it was extraordinary, though not finally heroic. One Sunday when my father came to town early, he saw the man of the family get off work and do some last-minute shopping for dinner, buying out of a few small shops and off the street vendors, as was common. He saw the man save buying the bread for last, but he had no space left in the basket attached to the bike's handlebars. The man did not hesitate. Tired and sweaty after a long day's work, he got back on his bicycle, stuck the long loaf of bread under his wet armpit, grabbed the handlebars, and biked off.

There my father was, just like me many years later, minding his own business, when this moment happened. There was no truck, exactly, but like me he got run over just the same. He had thought he had liked having dinner with this family, and that was the thing. Like me, he was having fun but getting run over at the same time.

His bread incident was just like my own story of getting run over. I didn't get hurt, exactly, though I did get to see the underside of something I thought I knew but didn't. My father and I, in our turn, got to see something new in the middle of what was absolutely familiar, which is the hardest place to see it. Neither of us ever forgot.

❀

Now it's my son's turn. This time it's Halloween night, but the big truck looms, even if none of us sees it clearly yet.

When my son was six and seven, he decided to go out on Halloween first as Sir Francis Drake and then as Hernán Cortés.

He would not waver on these choices. The next year he decided to go as Father Miguel Hidalgo, but my wife thought he
should go as a cow. A cow or a skeleton, but something people
recognize.

"But it's an educational opportunity," I said. She slugged me.

My son liked what was happening, and knew he was on to
something. "Don't take it, Dad," he said, egging me on.

"Well, maybe you could go as Father Hidalgo's cow," I suggested, sounding out what seemed like a compromise, and he
thought about it. But he caught on. He's in the gifted program.

"Maybe Father Hidal-cow," I said straight-faced, but I got
slugged again. I suggested to my wife that she should go as Sluggo.
I know she was not trying to stop him, but trying to help him, the
way my mother tried to help protect me by screaming when she
saw my father drive over me with that truck.

What I was really saying was, don't worry, but I didn't need
to. It was not hard to see that these people he chose to be were
from his books, stepping off their pages and into his life, into
all our lives. If just for a few hours, he was breathing as them.

The choices my son made were from his own insides, and
the evening was a lucky chance to give them voice, if only under the guise of entertainment and candy-grubbing. But when
the choices started to come from outside him, as they did after
this night, I knew what had happened.

Somehow in the last couple of years he has decided to take
the regular route. Embarrassment and ridicule, or at least blank
stares, have won out, at least for now. Last year he decided he
wanted to be maybe a ghost, with just a sheet and nothing else,
no decoration or drawing on it. Something totally invisible.
He wasn't even sure he wanted eye-holes, though he finally
gave in on that point.

The truck that has run over my son is slower than what
happened to me or my father. I've tried to take care of my son.
I've tried to tell him what I've been through. But I fear the
noise I make is like my mother's scream.

That's all there was to it, a simple enough change from one year to the next. But the Regular—that was the truck that loomed, and it has been as powerful as anything on the road. I saw it, but too late. He had been run over.

Still, I don't despair. I know he has seen something in the process, and will come out of it okay. He'll get out from under the truck, and in this business of his growing up I know he will see something of the truck's underside, something of its workings.

Some questions remain for me, however. Before my son changed his mind about his Halloween choices and was still willing to try, why did he choose Father Hidalgo and not a lesser-known pope, or for that matter, the inventor of fire or of squirt-guns? My son could not articulate very well why he chose this man or the others either, which gave us all some consternation. He simply knew that he was sure, and stuck to his choice through it all.

Perhaps it is because in some way he did not choose Father Hidalgo or Sir Francis Drake, or anyone else at all. Perhaps they chose him.

I don't mean this mysteriously, except inasmuch as learning is a mysterious process. He was not done with them yet, and this dressing up was one more attempt to get at something that words had not provided. And even when he decided he was done, and wanted to be a ghost instead, he probably wasn't done at all. But he had gotten a taste of some connection, and that is everything.

Astronomers have recently said that it is unexaggerated truth that we are star dust, that the carbon and oxygen and phosphorus in our bodies were created in the interiors of stars. Perhaps we hunger for something of those stars, for something more of ourselves in them. Perhaps they call to us. Maybe I heard something from them as I daydreamed as a little boy sitting in front of that truck. After all, there I sat, new, at the edge.

Perhaps I heard in the truck's engine the farthest lap of water, or saw in the truck's headlights the most distant spark of light, all reaching into this air, this thing, this experiment that was me. No one had yet told me I could not hear or see these things. I had no instruction manual at all, and so had to make up my own rules for the workings of the world.

❀

The truck's engine when I was so small, its headlights, my son's choice of costume, my father's epiphany as he stood on that corner in France—that each of these events might have had some life of their own that speaks to us, this is a hard thing to understand. Getting hit by a truck, either literally or figuratively, is hard to understand but not hard to remember, or to pay attention to.

My father's was a mature understanding, mine was a wide-eyed child's lack of understanding, and my son's experience was something between these two—we each learned something. But words can't articulate what that was. We each felt something, and that feeling was everything. We each made a connection to something big that words by themselves could not have made for us. We felt the moment, and that feeling was our dialogue.

"Are you all right?" my father asked me frantically as he pulled me out from under the truck. What he was really asking was whether or not I was injured—or worse. But was I all right? Getting run over by a truck, that's a lot of schooling in a very short moment. And school is good. I was all right. We just had to check if I was still alive.

My father. 1929–1995.